Google™ on the Go

Using an
Android-Powered
Mobile Phone

John Eddy
and
Patricia DiGiacomo Eddy

800 East 96th Street, Indianapolis, Indiana 46240 USA

Google on the Go: Using an Android-Powered Mobile Phone

ISBN-13: 978-0-7897-3953-7
ISBN-10: 0-7897-3953-4

Library of Congress Cataloging-in-Publication data is on file.

Printed in the United States of America

First Printing: February 2009

Trademarks

All terms mentioned in this book that are known to be trademarks or service marks have been appropriately capitalized. Que Publishing cannot attest to the accuracy of this information. Use of a term in this book should not be regarded as affecting the validity of any trademark or service mark.

Warning and Disclaimer

Every effort has been made to make this book as complete and as accurate as possible, but no warranty or fitness is implied. The information provided is on an "as is" basis. The authors and the publisher shall have neither liability nor responsibility to any person or entity with respect to any loss or damages arising from the information contained in this book.

Bulk Sales

Que Publishing offers excellent discounts on this book when ordered in quantity for bulk purchases or special sales. For more information, please contact

> **U.S. Corporate and Government Sales**
> **1-800-382-3419**
> **corpsales@pearsontechgroup.com**

For sales outside the United States, please contact

> **International Sales**
> **international@pearson.com**

Associate Publisher
Greg Wiegand

Acquisitions Editor
Laura Norman

Development Editor
Todd Brakke

Managing Editor
Patrick Kanouse

Senior Project Editor
Tonya Simpson

Copy Editor
Gayle Johnson

Indexer
Ken Johnson

Proofreader
Williams Woods Publishing
Servic es

Technical Editor
Christian Kenyeres

Publishing Coordinator
Cindy Teeters

Book Designer
Anne Jones

Compositor
Bronkella Publishing

Contents at a Glance

Contents

About the Authors

John Eddy is a gadget hobbyist who infuriates his wife by continually getting new toys that need to be put somewhere. The majority of his career has been spent trying to ensure that normal, everyday people can successfully use their technological wonders. He has helped people both directly, through product support, and indirectly, by moderating online forums and newsgroups, thus ensuring a safe environment in which to seek answers.

After his long career in and around Microsoft, it's ironic that John's first book is about Google. He spends his days and nights in the Seattle area reading, watching too much TV and not enough movies, and enjoying quality time on his Xbox 360 and Wii with his far more tech-savvy wife. Author of *Special Edition Using Microsoft Office Outlook 2007*, she shares his love of cooking and eating. Their food chronicles can be found at www.cooklocal.com.

Patricia DiGiacomo Eddy is an accomplished technology author and mobile phone geek who isn't nearly as infuriated with her husband's love of gadgets as he might think. She has written several books, including *Special Edition Using Microsoft Office Outlook 2003*, *Special Edition Using Microsoft Office Outlook 2007*, *Absolute Beginner's Guide to OneNote*, and *Access 2003: VBA Programmer's Reference*. Her day job is spent writing about email technology with a major software company. Her evenings are spent writing about a wide variety of other topics, including health and fitness, cooking, and Seattle culture. She enjoys a good game of Wii Tennis. Although she watches too much TV, she isn't planning on changing that habit any time soon. Patricia and her husband recently completed their first half marathon and are looking forward to training for a full marathon as soon as this book is on the shelves.

Dedication

To my wife, without whom none of this would have happened, or happened so well.

To everyone else, you can wait for the next book to get something dedicated to you.

—John Eddy

To my husband, who can make the worst days infinitely better simply by being there, and who makes the best days even more extraordinary than they already are.

—Patricia DiGiacomo Eddy

Acknowledgments

First and foremost, I need to acknowledge my wife for more reasons than I can count. Without her assistance, I never would have written this book, or if I had, I'd likely have given up upon first receiving constructive criticism.

I'd like to thank my acquisitions editor, Laura Norman, and development editor, Todd Brakke, whose constructive criticism I've been largely protected from by my wife. She swears by you, so I guess I should as well. Christian Kenyeres double-checked all our facts and helped us ensure that the parts of the chapters written at 2 a.m. were as clear and easy to read as the parts of the chapters written at 6 p.m. Our copy editor, Gayle Johnson, helped ensure that the computer's spell checker didn't substitute the word fore for four and double-checked all our content for the utmost clarity. Thanks also to all the other folks at Que who helped make this book possible.

Thanks to Great Big Sea, Eddie From Ohio, The Gourds, Todd Snider, Richard Cheese, and whoever else scrolled through my playlist, driving me forward.

Last, I'd like to thank everyone who put up with me while I wrote this book—friends, family, and coworkers alike. (Special thanks to the folks at Twitter for giving me a way to vent quickly, cleanly, and succinctly.)

—John Eddy

Of course, I'd like to thank my husband, who did the lion's share of the writing of this book. I'd also like to thank a few friends who helped keep me sane during the crunch time for the book—namely, Maureen, Ben, and Danny and Yvette, who came to town on vacation and proceeded to cook for us one night just so we could keep working to meet our deadlines.

—Patricia DiGiacomo Eddy

We Want to Hear from You!

As the reader of this book, *you* are our most important critic and commentator. We value your opinion and want to know what we're doing right, what we could do better, what areas you'd like to see us publish in, and any other words of wisdom you're willing to pass our way.

As an associate publisher for Que Publishing, I welcome your comments. You can email or write me directly to let me know what you did or didn't like about this book—as well as what we can do to make our books better.

Please note that I cannot help you with technical problems related to the topic of this book. We do have a User Services group, however, where I will forward specific technical questions related to the book.

When you write, please be sure to include this book's title and author as well as your name, email address, and phone number. I will carefully review your comments and share them with the author and editors who worked on the book.

Email: feedback@quepublishing.com

Mail: Greg Wiegand
        Associate Publisher
        Que Publishing
        800 East 96th Street
        Indianapolis, IN 46240 USA

Reader Services

Visit our website and register this book at informit.com/register for convenient access to any updates, downloads, or errata that might be available for this book.

Introduction

Who Is This Book For?

I'd love to say that this book is for you, no matter who you are. But no one book could cover the wide range of cell phone users when it comes to discussing a new system.

So, how do you know if this book is for you?

Maybe all you've ever used a standard mobile phone for is making phone calls. Maybe you occasionally send a text message or use your cell phone camera to share pictures with friends. Maybe you'd like to jump ahead to the latest phone software, but you feel a little nervous about that.

If that sounds like you, I'm writing for you.

However, if you're constantly buying new technologies and skipping the user's manual, preferring to play with what you've purchased and figure it out for yourself, you can still use this book as a handy quick reference to a feature that you forgot how to configure.

If you're already planning what software you can write for Android, this probably isn't the right book. We give you pointers to some resources to help you write software, but this topic is not discussed in depth.

What Is the Open Handset Alliance?

The Open Handset Alliance (OHA) is a group of companies that looked at the current generation of mobile phones and decided that only by coming together could they best drive innovation and give customers a better experience when it comes to their mobile phones.

These companies range from hardware manufacturers such as HTC, LG Electronics, Motorola, and Samsung, to mobile operators such as T-Mobile and Sprint Nextel, to software companies such as Google and eBay.

What Is Android?

Mobile phones, like your computer, have an operating system. It can be something simple, with few to no graphics and no color, that just allows you to make phone calls. Or it could be extremely powerful, letting you do almost everything you can do with your desktop computer.

Android is an operating system for your mobile phone and definitely falls into the second category. Not only does Android offer you a powerful Internet experience, but tools are also provided via the Internet to let people write their own applications for the phone.

In addition to Internet connectivity and programmability, Android has been released under the Apache v2 open-source license.

What Does Open Source Mean?

Open source has a number of different definitions, and admittedly, this particular section could sound a little techy. So let's try a basic explanation:

Open source means that the words behind the software are available for anyone to read and improve.

If you want to understand more, keep reading. Otherwise, skip to the next section.

Software, such as Windows and Halo, is written with simple words. Those words are run through something called a compiler that takes those words that you and I can read (to varying degrees of understanding) and makes them something that computers can read and use.

What this means all depends on what license is used. Just as a driver's license lets you drive, and a hunting license lets you hunt, different open-source licenses let people do different things. Some require you to take changes you might make to the software and share them by putting the changes back into the software that other people will download.

The Apache v2 license allows the people making the phones and the mobile phone service providers to make changes to the software without having to provide those changes to the other manufacturers.

G1 Features

When this book was written, only one mobile phone was available that was running the Android operating system. The G1 is manufactured by HTC and is available from T-Mobile.

Although your phone might look different, the G1 appears in figures throughout this book, so I thought a quick look at the phone would be a good idea.

This particular phone has a touch screen, a camera, and a slide-out keyboard. The front of the phone is shown in Figure I.1.

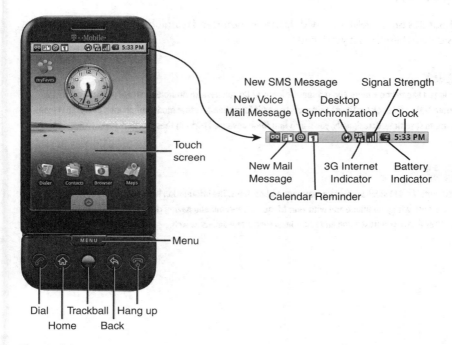

Figure I.1
The T-Mobile G1.

The Hang-up button disconnects any active calls and locks the device. It is also the button you use to power the device off and on.

In fact, before we go into the phone itself, if you haven't turned on the device yet, why don't you do that now? Just hold down the Hang-up button to turn on the device.

About This Book

We start by covering the basic functions that you'll use with just about any mobile phone. If you're unfamiliar with basic phone features, Chapter 1 is a must-read.

After that we'll follow with some of the features that make an Android-powered phone so interesting. You can access your Google Calendar, read your email, and use the phone as a personal media player (an MP3 player). Browsing the Web is easy, and you can even add applications to your phone. One of our favorites allows you to use the phone's camera to scan a barcode and quickly find out who has the best price on the item, both locally and on the Web.

If you fancy yourself a programmer (either amateur or professional), you can even write programs for your phone.

Getting the 411

Throughout this book, we've included tips, tricks, notes, and warnings. When you see the following sidebars, here's what you'll find.

Would you like to know more about a specific feature? Do you have an Android-powered phone that's not a G1 from T-Mobile? Look for The 411 sidebars to find information on other models of phones, or tips that you can use to save time. Occasionally, you'll also find some advanced tricks in these sections.

Watch out! The 911 sidebars contain warnings and cautions. The information here will help keep you out of trouble, both with your phone and with your friends. We recommend paying close attention to these sidebars. They'll save you frustration and sometimes even a few dollars as well.

The Phone Basics

Setting Up the Phone

When you first start up the phone, you'll find that, unless you only want to call emergency services or you just enjoy staring at the Android logo, you're required to associate your phone with a Google account. If you don't have a Google account yet, you can set one up from the phone itself.

In the case of the G1, you are asked to touch the Android logo. Then you see a brief screen describing the need for the Google account. After reviewing the page, touch Next. You can choose whether to use an existing Google account or create a new one.

Using an Existing Google Account

If you already have a Google account, simply touch the Sign In button. Enter your username and password, and then touch the Sign In button again.

That's really all there is to getting started using an existing Google account. You should receive a notification that your account is now associated with the phone, unless you typed the wrong password. In that case, you are told that you typed the wrong password, and you have to retype it. If everything is set up properly, the phone notifies you that your Google account is now linked.

Creating a New Google Account

You need to create a Google account if you don't already have one, or if you just want to start fresh with a new account. (We'll show you how to switch from one account to another in the section, "Resetting Your Phone," in Chapter 13.

No matter why you might want to do it, it's easy to configure a new Google account with your phone by following these steps:

1. Tap the **Create** button.

2. Enter the appropriate data in the **First name**, **Last name**, and **Username** fields. Tap **Next**.

3. If your choice of a username is unavailable, you can type in a new username or select from some automatically generated alternatives.

4. Either enter a new name or pick one from the alternative list by touching the visible alternative and then sliding your finger up and down the list to scroll through it. Tap the alternative you'd like to use, and then tap **Next**.

5. Enter a password, and set up a security question to answer if you forget your password in the future. When you're done, tap **Create**.

Your password needs to be eight characters long at a minimum. A good password is a mix of uppercase and lowercase letters, isn't a real word, and has both numbers and special characters in addition to letters. The password aaaaaaa% is a weak password, whereas Th3_g0VrD5! is a strong password. If you choose a password that's too weak, you'll be asked to enter a different one later in the setup process.

6. Read through the Google Terms of Service, and then touch **I agree**. Tap **Next**. (If you don't agree, you might want to return the phone, because without the Google account, your Android-powered phone will only be able to make emergency calls.)

7. After the phone communicates with Google's servers, you're presented with a CAPTCHA. Enter the text displayed, and touch **Next**.

A CAPTCHA is a method that's used to differentiate between a person and a computer. You're presented with a series of characters that you need to input. The characters are fuzzy or distorted enough that a computer wouldn't be able to be programmed to read them. So if they are entered correctly, a human is most likely at the keyboard. If you can't read the CAPTCHA, or if you can't read all the characters, you're given a different set of characters to try to translate. There doesn't appear to be a limit on the number of mistakes you can make, so don't feel bad if you don't get it on the first try.

But wait, you might be wondering why you would need to differentiate between a person and a computer. Well, perhaps you want to try to grab a whole lot of user names at once, just so other people couldn't get them. You might write a program that would try to create all those accounts for you. We aren't just talking about five or six, but hundreds at once. That's what CAPTCHA tries to prevent.

8. If you end up back on the password selection screen, the password you selected proba-
    bly was too weak. Choose a stronger password, and tap **Next**.

9. Touch **Finish**, and your initial setup is complete!

Navigating the Phone's Screens

Although the steps to set up the phone are pretty self-explanatory, navigating the phone
needs a bit of a walkthrough.

Keep in mind that the screen on the phone will turn off after a bit, so if the screen goes black,
press the Menu button. The Menu button is very important, because it often gives you access
to extra commands, depending on what you're doing at the time.

When looking at the phone's main screen, shown in Figure 1.1, you'll find an analog clock near
the top of the screen, below the Notification bar, and four icons at the bottom labeled Dialer,
Contacts, Browser, and Maps. Below that is a gray manila folder tab called the Application tab.

Figure 1.1
*The main screen of the
G1.*

4.1.1

If you're using a phone other than the T-Mobile G1, your home screen might look a little different.

If you touch the screen and slide your finger to the right, you'll likely end up on a blank
screen, as shown in Figure 1.2.

Figure 1.2
You can add shortcuts to this screen.

Okay, sure, it isn't entirely blank. You still have the Application tab and the Notification bar. There isn't much to see here, so touch the screen and slide your finger to the left to return to the home screen, and then slide to the left again to see the screen shown in Figure 1.3.

Figure 1.3
The Search screen.

You still have the Application tab and the mostly omnipresent Notification bar, but on this screen, you also see the Google search box.

Now that your finger is used to the movement, put your finger on the Application tab (it should turn orange) and drag your finger to the top of the screen to display all the applications, as shown in Figure 1.4.

Figure 1.4
The Application tab expands to show all your applications.

All these icons represent the applications installed on the phone. You can simply tap an icon to start the application. If you happen to get lost and want to get back to the main screen, just give the Home button a quick press.

Near the top of the screen is an icon for Calculator. If you touch this icon, your classic-looking calculator starts. So, do what everyone with a new calculator does, and verify that 2+2 still equals 4. After you're sure that it does, press the Home button again to move back to the home screen.

While you're experimenting with controls, the phone used for this book also has a trackball. Although it is cool in a Missile Command sort of way, it isn't necessarily as convenient as the touch screen. But, because it's there, take a few minutes to give it a spin just to familiarize yourself with how it works. Note that not only is it a trackball, but it clicks. If you spin the trackball down to the Application tab and click the trackball, you'll find that it slides out the tab, just like using the touch screen.

Making and Answering Calls

You have a nice little piece of plastic and electronics in your hand, but it comes down to a modern-day equivalent of Alexander Graham Bell's (or Antonio Meucci's) harmonic telegraph. Let's look at the basics of making a call.

If you have a phone with a slide-out keyboard, or a keypad, simply press the Home key and start dialing using the numeric keys. Press the green handset button to connect the call.

Most mobile phones have a green handset button somewhere on the left side of the phone. Your phone might have a button with a picture of a telephone handset, but the button could also say Dial, Send, Connect, or something similar.

If your phone utilizes a touch screen like the G1, follow these steps to place a call:

1. Press the green **handset** button.

2. Tap the **Dialer** tab, as shown in Figure 1.5.

Figure 1.5
Use the dialer to make calls.

3. Enter the phone number of the person you want to call.

4. Press the green **handset** button again.

To answer a call, press the green handset button. There is no way to use the touch screen to answer an incoming call.

Speakerphone

After you've placed a call, you might not want to walk or sit around with the phone pressed up against your ear. Maybe someone who's with you wants to talk to whoever you're calling.

As soon as you're done dialing, or any time after that, you can press the Menu button and touch Speaker, shown in Figure 1.6, to turn on the speakerphone. If you want to turn it off, simply repeat those same steps.

Figure 1.6
Turn the speakerphone on and off.

Conference Calling

Party calling, conference calling, and multiple-party calling all refer to connecting three people on the same call. Whatever you want to call it, setting it up is easy:

1. Call the first person.

2. After the first call is connected, press the **Menu** button and tap **Add Call**.

3. Dial the next person's number. After you're connected, press the **Menu** button and tap **Merge calls**.

Call Waiting

Let's say you're one of the cool cats and not only do you get one person to call you, you get two. At the same time, no less. While you're talking on the phone. You hear a couple beeps to let you know that a call is incoming. On the screen, you also see a display to show you who is calling, as shown in Figure 1.7.

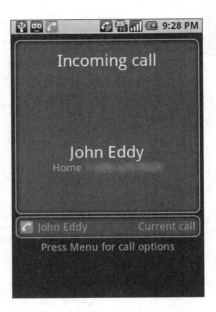

Figure 1.7
You've got a second call!

At that point, as the screen says, press the Menu button for one of two options:

- Hold call in progress & answer. This option places the current call on hold and lets you answer the incoming call. You can either finish the incoming call and then go back to your first call, or you can conference the calls, talking to both people at once.

- End call in progress & answer. This option hangs up on your current call and answers the incoming call.

Configuring Calling Features

One of the beautiful things about mobile phones is the wide variety of features available for free, such as call waiting and conference calling. You might have to pay for these on your home phone. Your phone allows you to configure a wide variety of these features, through the Application tab.

Expand the Application tab right now by tapping it. Look for the Settings icon. If you don't see it, simply touch the screen and slide your finger up until you see the Settings icon, as shown in Figure 1.8.

Tap the Settings icon, and then tap Call settings to display the screen shown in Figure 1.9.

Figure 1.8
The Settings icon is at the bottom of the Applications tab.

Figure 1.9
You can configure a variety of call settings on your phone.

Fixed Dialing Number

Fixed dialing is a feature in which a mobile phone is allowed to dial only certain numbers. This can be helpful if you want to give your teenager a mobile phone but you want her to be able to call only you, not all her friends. This particular feature is a bit more advanced than we plan on discussing in this book, so if you want more information about it, contact your mobile phone provider.

Voicemail

We'll talk more about voicemail in a bit, but this particular entry in Call settings simply configures what phone number corresponds to your Voicemail box. It should be set by default by your mobile phone provider and can be ignored here.

Call Forwarding

Call forwarding is a great feature that allows you to, well, do exactly that—automatically forward incoming calls to various locations based on what is happening with your phone at the moment.

These settings are actually stored with your mobile provider. Your phone retrieves them whenever you want to view the settings. Any changes you make are sent back to your mobile provider when you're done. Tap Call forwarding to open the call forwarding settings, as shown in Figure 1.10.

Figure 1.10
There are a variety of call forwarding options.

411

If you're in an area of spotty service, you might have trouble pulling up the settings from your mobile provider. Just wait until you have a strong signal, and try again.

You can configure call forwarding with the following options:

- **Always forward:** This is disabled by default, because it prevents any calls from reaching your phone.

- **Forward when busy:** If you're on the phone when a new call comes in, this is the phone number your caller is redirected to. Normally this is your voicemail number, and most of the time you won't have a reason to change it.

- **Forward when unanswered:** Just like forward when busy, this is the number that your calls are redirected to if you don't answer.

You probably won't use the Forward when unanswered option very often, but it can be helpful when you know you won't be able to answer your phone. You could use it when you're at a conference or on a business trip.

- **Forward when unreachable:** This is the number that your callers are redirected to when your mobile phone is turned off or doesn't have service. You might want to set this to another phone number if you're planning a trip where you know you won't have mobile phone coverage.

Caller ID

Caller ID shows you the phone number of the person calling you so that you can decide whether to take the call. But this feature has another purpose. If you want to hide your phone number when you call someone, click Additional call settings, and select Caller ID, where you have three options:

- **Network default:** The default number from your mobile phone service provider.
- **Hide number:** Hides your number from the person you are calling.
- **Show number:** Shows your number to the person you are calling.

Call Waiting

Earlier we discussed how call waiting works. To turn it on or off, use the Additional call settings screen, as shown in Figure 1.11. If it's checked, you're alerted to new calls when you're on the phone with someone.

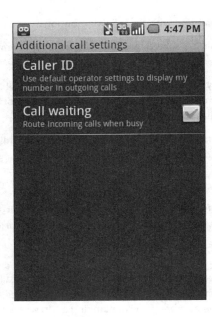

Figure 1.11
You can turn call waiting on and off.

If it isn't checked, inbound calls roll straight to voicemail if you're on the phone.

Operator Selection

There are advanced subjects, and then there are *advanced* subjects. This is one of the latter and isn't discussed here. In some countries, you can choose from several mobile operators on the same phone. However, that isn't very common. Contact your mobile phone provider for more information.

Managing Voicemail

All mobile phone plans come with voicemail. Even though your mobile phone company does the basic setup of your voicemail, there are still options you need to configure through your mobile phone.

To set up your voicemail, pull up the dialer as discussed in the "Making and Answering Calls" section, and touch and hold 1 until the phone dials. At that point, you need to listen to the voice prompts that your mobile service provider gives you, because they are different for every provider and are subject to change. At this point you can choose an outgoing message or record your own. Follow the prompts to rerecord, or save the message and complete the voicemail setup process.

When you receive a voicemail message, the notification bar at the top of the screen displays the New voicemail icon, as shown in Figure 1.12. You can access your voicemail through the dialer, by touching and holding 1, or by pulling down the notifications bar and touching the New voicemail icon.

Voicemail Notification Icon

Figure 1.12

The voicemail notification icon appears in the notification bar.

Date/Time Settings and Alarms

I've noticed that I rarely wear a watch anymore. Why is this? Well, it's because I always have my mobile phone with me. Why wear a watch when I can just whip out my phone and check the time? The next few sections show you how to manage the clock on your phone and set some alarms.

Setting the Date and Time

Most phones and providers these days obtain the date and time from the mobile phone operator. However, you might want to change the time. Maybe you want to set your phone to the time zone your sister lives in, or maybe you want to set the clock 5 minutes fast so that you're always on time. To set the date and time, follow these steps:

1. If you aren't on the main screen, press the **Home** key.

2. Press the **Menu** button, and tap **Settings**.

3. Scroll through the screen, and tap **Date & time** to bring up the Date & time settings screen, as shown in Figure 1.13.

4. If **Automatic** is checked, uncheck it so that you can change your date and time settings independent of your mobile phone operator. You' see options for changing the date, time zone, and time.

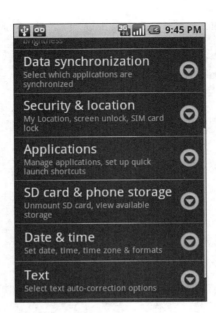

You'll notice two other options available to you on the Date & time settings screen:

- **Use 24-hour format:** Unfortunately, this won't make Jack Bauer show up when you're in trouble; it only switches the clock between showing 1:00 p.m. and 13:00.

- **Select date format:** If you're more comfortable reading the date in a different format, this is where you configure it.

Setting an Alarm

Personally, I never understood the usefulness of wake-up calls. Most hotel rooms have a digital alarm clock. But if you're worried about the power going out, your mobile phone lets you set your own alarm. Several alarms are actually preconfigured (though not turned on), but we'll create a new one for this exercise. To set an alarm, follow these steps:

1. Tap to display the **Application** tab, and touch the **Alarm Clock** icon.

2. Press the **Menu** button to display the Alarm Clock menu.

3. Tap the **Add alarm** icon to display the screen shown in Figure 1.14.

The following alarm options are available:

- **Alarm:** This is the toggle that enables or disables the alarm. A green check mark means that the alarm will go off. Don't see one? The alarm is disabled and won't go off. Simply tap the Alarm line to toggle the check mark on and off. When you touch it, a pop-up shows you how long it will be until the alarm will go off.

Figure 1.14
*Use this screen to config-
ure a new alarm.*

- **Time:** This is when you want the alarm to go off.
- **Ringtone:** Despite the fact that your phone can play many different audio formats (more on that later) and comes with quite a few ringtones, only six options are available (see Figure 1.15).

Figure 1.15
*Choose the sound for
your alarm.*

- **Vibrate:** Vibrate is simply a toggle. If it is checked in green, the phone will vibrate when the alarm goes off.

- **Repeat:** You can configure the alarm to go off on certain days, as shown in Figure 1.16. If you do not select anything on this screen, the alarm goes off only once, when the clock hits whatever time is set on the Time option.

Figure 1.16

Choose the days on which the alarm will go off.

If you'd like to change the settings of an existing alarm, click the left side of the alarm, rather than the check mark, to get to the options.

After you've made the settings you want, you can press the Back button to go back to the list of alarms. But, before you do that, why not set an alarm to go off in about 5 minutes, based on the time on the Notification bar? Also enable the alarm so that you can see the best feature of the Alarm Clock.

Snooze

Could there be a more wonderful invention than the snooze alarm? How could you not like a feature that makes an alarm go away for 10 minutes?

Like any good alarm clock, this one comes with a snooze button. Simply tap the Snooze button when the alarm goes off.

Be sure you're awake enough to be able to discern the Snooze button from the Disable button. If you tap Disable, the alarm will not go off again.

Deleting an Alarm

Deleting an alarm is easy. Simply tap the alarm to view the settings, press the Menu button, and then tap Delete alarm. How easy is that?

Text Messaging

"f U cn rED DIS, U problE dun nEd 2 rED DIS sectN." (Translated: If you can read this, you probably don't need to read this section.)

Text messaging is all the rage. It's an easy, fast, simple way to send a blurb to someone (provided that he has a mobile phone too) without interrupting him with a phone call. Just don't try to do it while driving. Not only is it dangerous, it's illegal in some states. Don't do it in a movie theatre, either; that glowing screen is really annoying.

Sending a Text Message

To send a text message, follow these steps:

1. From the **Home** screen, open the **Application** tab.

2. Open the **Messaging** application by tapping the icon. If you can't see the icon, touch the screen and drag up (or down) until you see it.

3. Tap **New message**, and slide open the keyboard (if needed).

4. In the **To** box of the compose form, type the phone number of the person you want to send a message to. Keep in mind that some people have to pay for inbound messages, so you probably don't want to text someone without making sure it's okay first.

5. Tap the **Type to compose, press Enter to send** field, and type the message you'd like to send. You need to keep it short—text messages are limited to 160 characters.

6. When you're ready to send your message, you can press the **Enter** key, or touch the **Send** button on the screen.

Configuring Text Messaging Alert Settings

Great! You've sent a text message. You could stare at your phone, waiting for the person to text you back, or you could configure your other messaging settings.

To configure text messaging alert settings, follow these steps:

1. Open **Settings**, either through the **Application** tab or by pressing the **Menu** button while on the Home screen.

2. Tap **sound & display**, and then tap **Notification ringtone**.

3. Choose the ringtone you'd like to use. Tapping each ringtone will play it so that you can hear it before you decide.

In addition to playing your chosen ringtone, when you receive a new text message, you'll also see the new message notification on the Notification bar.

Viewing a Received Message

If your friends and family text you back, you need to know how to view received messages. There are a few different ways to see a message you've received.

If you're still looking at the screen where you sent the message, as shown in Figure 1.17, you just see the message right there.

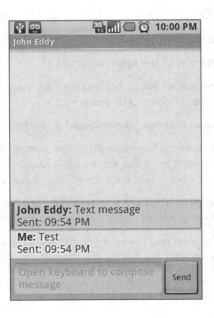

Figure 1.17
Text messages you've sent and received.

If you're looking at the home screen (or your phone is in your pocket and you pull it out when you hear the notification sound), look at the Notification bar at the top of the screen. Tap the Notification bar and drag your finger down to display your notifications, as shown in Figure 1.18. Tap the notification for the text message to read the message.

Figure 1.18
You can tap the message notification to open the message.

Customizing Your Phone

You don't want your phone to be like everyone else's. You want pizzazz! Flair! You want to customize your phone to be uniquely you. You've already seen some of the notification settings you can customize, but let's go back in and take a closer look.

Sound Settings

To customize the sound settings on your phone, follow these steps:

1. Press the **Menu** button, and tap **Settings**.

2. Tap **Sound & display** to bring up the screen shown in Figure 1.19.

You can customize a wide variety of settings:

- **Silent mode:** You can turn silent mode on or off. When this is checked, the only noise your phone will make is when it plays audio or video files. When silent mode is checked, you can't customize any other settings.

Figure 1.19
You can customize a variety of sound settings.

- **Ringer volume:** You might have seen a smaller version of this screen just by accidentally hitting the rocker button on the left side of the phone. You'll notice that the phone beeps as you lift your finger from picking a volume, just to give you an idea of how loud the phone will be when ringing. Touch OK if you want the volume changed to what you picked; touch Cancel if not.

- **Media volume:** The media volume functions the same as the Ringer volume feature, but it controls the volume of any music or video files you might want to play.

- **Phone ringtone:** This is a list of ringtones that you have available. When you select a ringtone, it plays for you until you touch either another ringtone, OK, or Cancel.

- **Phone vibrate:** When this option is checked, the phone vibrates as well as plays the chosen ringtone when you get a call. However, the phone also has a Vibrate Only mode if you don't want to hear the ringtone. If Silent mode is checked, the phone won't vibrate or play a ringtone.

- **Notification ringtone:** This is the ringtone that's played when you receive a new message.

- **Audible touch tones:** This setting applies only to the on-screen dial pad that you get when making a phone call. If you enjoy hearing "Mary Had a Little Lamb" when you dial 3 2 1 2 3 3 3 2 2 2 3 9 9 3 2 1 2 3 3 3 3 2 2 3 2 1, you can turn this on.

- **Audible selection:** When turned on, this setting produces a little "click" sound every time you touch an icon.

Display Settings

You can access two Display settings from the same screen as the Sound settings:

- **Brightness:** The Brightness slider controls how bright the screen is. Remember, the brighter the screen, the less battery life you'll have.

- **Screen timeout:** This option controls how long it takes between your last touch of the screen or one of the buttons and the screen turning off to conserve battery life.

Autocorrect Options

If you tap Settings from the Application tab, you'll find a section labeled Text settings, as shown in Figure 1.20. You see the basic autocorrect settings that your phone will do for you.

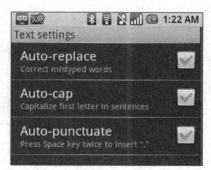

Figure 1.20
Autocorrect. Because we can't always be brilliant.

Three basic options can help you with your typing skills:

- **Auto-replace:** This corrects some mistyped words. Although your phone can't change "gturbf" to "friend," just because your fingers were on the wrong keys, it can change some common errors for you, such as "teh" to "the."

- **Auto-cap:** As the name says, this option automatically capitalizes the first letter in a sentence.

- **Auto-punctuate:** If you press the spacebar twice, this option autoinserts a period for you and removes one of the spaces. At some point since I went through typing class, the world moved from requiring two spaces between sentences to only one. Unfortunately, I didn't get the memo, much to the annoyance of many editors.

These settings should be used anywhere that you type, be it web forms, email messages, SMS messages, or notes.

Customizing Your Home Screen

Some people prefer to keep their home screen nice and neat and looking exactly like it did the day they bought their phone. There's nothing wrong with that. However, if you want to play around with your phone a bit and change its look, there are several ways you can customize your phone.

Wallpaper

Whether you have the G1 from T-Mobile or some other Android-powered phone, your home screen has some visually stimulating wallpaper that serves as the background for your phone. You can change this wallpaper to another graphic or even to a picture that you've taken with the phone's camera.

Tap and hold the screen—but not on an icon or the clock or search box. You see something like the screen shown in Figure 1.21.

Figure 1.21
There's no place like home.

Tap Wallpaper. As shown in Figure 1.22, you have two options of what to put on your home screen. You can select a picture from your phone, either one that you've taken or any you've added, or you can choose from one of the Wallpaper gallery of wallpapers that are already on your phone.

Perfect for personalizing your phone just the way you want it.

➜   For more information on taking pictures, **see** Chapter 5, "Taking Pictures with Your Phone."

Feel free to change your wallpaper as often as you want.

Figure 1.22
Wallpaper doesn't have to be tacky.

Shortcuts

You can access more options by tapping and holding the home screen. We'll cover applications in Chapter 9, "Adding New Applications," but tap Shortcuts now. Shortcuts are an easy way to get to something on your phone. What sorts of things? Let's take a look at Figure 1.23 and go through the list.

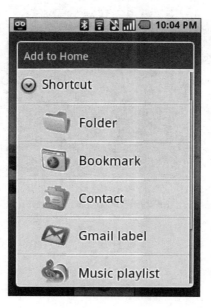

Figure 1.23
A smorgasboard of shortcut options.

- **Folder:** This is just a container for icons. If you don't want to fill up your home screen, create a folder and throw the icons in it. Don't worry that every folder will be called Folder. Just open a folder, tap and hold the Folder bar at the top, and you'll get the option to rename the folder.

- **Bookmark:** Any bookmarks you've created can be added to your desktop with just a click. Tap the bookmark and you open the web page without needing to open the web browser.

- **Contact:** Whatever contact you pick gets added to your home screen. If you specified a picture for the contact, that picture is the icon. Tapping it just opens the contact.

- **Gmail label:** If you've created labels, you can drag them to the desktop, giving you simple tap access to get directly to that label.

- **Music playlist:** If you've set up some playlists, this is a great way to get directly into them. Perfect access to the perfect set of tunes.

To actually create the shortcut, just tap the type of shortcut you want to create. We'll assume that you've already created a couple of contacts, so tap Contact to display Figure 1.24.

Figure 1.24
You can create a shortcut to any of your contacts.

After you've chosen the contact, the shortcut appears on your home screen, as shown in Figure 1.25.

Shortcut to Contact Record

Figure 1.25
We created a shortcut to John Eddy's contact record.

But wait—there's more! You can also add some widgets to your home screen.

Widgets

Remember when a widget was a term used in economics classes to talk about something a company made without having to come up with an actual product? Widgets nowadays, in computer terms, describe small programs that do little things.

Right now, as shown in Figure 1.26, there are only three lonely widgets, two of which you've already seen on the home screen.

The Clock and the Search box you've already seen. In fact, if you wanted to get rid of them, that would be easy enough. Just tap, hold, and drag and drop the widget onto the trash can. You can always add it back to whichever screen you want if you change your mind.

The Picture frame option is new. It allows you to put a picture on your home screen. This option is different from the Wallpaper option.

Tap Picture frame, tap the picture you'd like to have on your desktop, and crop the picture. You end up with a picture on your desktop, as shown in Figure 1.27.

Figure 1.26
By the time you get your phone, there may be more widgets than this.

Figure 1.27
A reminder that into every life, a little monkey must fall.

411

You'll likely have to crop the picture so that it fits within the Picture frame. The Picture frame is necessarily small so that it doesn't take up the entire home screen. So if you want the entire picture to fit within the frame, you need to start with a pretty small picture.

➔   For more information on taking and cropping pictures, **see** Chapter 5, "Taking Pictures with Your Phone."

Working with Contacts

What Are Contacts?

A contact is someone you email, text, instant message (IM) with, or talk to on your phone. You can connect to these people quickly from your mobile phone.

If you're using an existing Google account, all your contacts from Gmail are automatically downloaded to your phone to make it easier for you to call, email, text message, and instant message them. If this isn't your first mobile phone, or if you've played around with your phone a bit already, you've probably discovered this feature. This chapter walks you through creating contacts, using them, and keeping them organized.

Viewing Your Contacts

You have a few different ways to access your contacts.

On your computer, you can pull them up by opening your browser and going to www.gmail.com, signing in, and clicking Contacts, as shown in Figure 2.1.

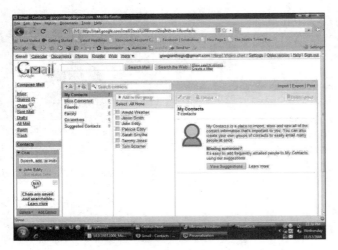

Figure 2.1
You can access your contacts from your computer.

On your phone, however, you have a number of different ways to access your contacts:

- Tap the Contacts icon on the home screen.
- Open the Applications tab, and tap Contacts.
- Open the Dialer, and tap the Contacts tab, as shown in Figure 2.2.

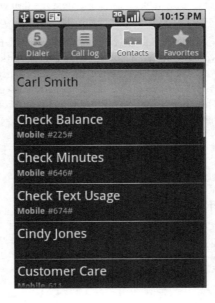

Figure 2.2
Tap the Contacts tab from the Dialer.

If you have a lot of contacts, you might find scrolling up and down through the list a little tedious. As you scroll, you'll see a little quick index tab slide out from the right side of the screen. Pick your finger up off the screen, touch that tab, and scroll by the first letter of the display name. You can also slide open the keyboard and start typing the first or last name of whoever you're trying to find.

Wow. Those are a lot of ways to see your contacts.

Now that you can see your contacts, you have a couple of ways to display them on the screen.

When you're looking at your list of contacts, press the Menu button and touch Display group. The options are fairly self-evident; however, if you go to your Gmail account in a web browser, you can set up groups of contacts. Those groups will be listed here as well.

You can create groups of contacts from your computer. Just log in to Gmail, click Contacts, and then click the New Group button. Name your group, and then you can add any of your existing contacts or a new contact to the group. I have a group for all my family members so when I need to send out an announcement or a group email, I can select the group instead of selecting each person individually.

Now that you see your contacts, what can you do with them?

Adding a New Contact

If you started with a new Google account, if you want to create a new contact to add to your existing list, or if you happen to have a Google account with no contacts, you need to know how to create a new contact.

Because we were just looking at Contacts, let's go through the steps of how to add a new contact from there:

1. Press the **Menu** button and tap **New contact** to display the New contact field, shown in Figure 2.3.

2. Type the first and last names of the person you'd like to add in the **New contact** field.

3. Enter the person's phone number in the **Dial number** field. This is the number that will be dialed by default when you select the contact.

4. Touch the **Mobile** box to change the Dial number category from Mobile to Work, Home, or Other if necessary.

5. Enter the contact's email address in the **Send email** field. As with the phone number, you can change the label attached to the email address to Work, Home, or Other.

Figure 2.3
You can add a lot of information about a contact.

6. The next field is the contact's ringtone. You can specify a different ringtone for each of your contacts. Tap the **Ringtone** button to select a ringtone.

7. If you don't want to talk to the contact, tap to check the box **Send calls directly to voicemail**. Just be aware that after you check this box, you can't answer a call from this contact unless you uncheck this box first.

8. The **More info** box is where you enter multiple phone numbers, physical addresses, IM addresses, or even birthday and anniversary information.

9. Tap the **Save** button to save your contact.

That's all there is to it. You've just created a new contact.

Editing an Existing Contact

If you had an existing Google account with contacts, those names and email addresses will already be stored on your mobile phone. If you need to store more information about your contact, or if you need to change something in a contact, follow these steps to edit an existing contact:

1. Press the **Menu** button and tap **Edit contact** (or touch and hold your finger on the contact and then touch **Edit contact** on the pop-up menu).

2. Tap the **More Info** button. You have five groups of labels to select from:

    •   **Phone:** The phone labels available are the same ones you see when you create a new contact. The Other label allows you to create your own label, such as "Dad's Vacation Home in Reno."

- **Email:** The email labels are the same ones available when you create a new contact. As with the phone labels, you can create your own custom label.

- **IM:** If your contact has an IM address, you can specify it here.

- **Postal Address:** It probably comes as no surprise that this option lets you put in a postal address of either the Home, Work, Other, or Custom variety.

- **Other:** Other provides two options, Organization and Note. Organization allows you to input a company name and position title. Note lets you add some notes to the contact.

3. To save your changes, press the **Menu** button and touch **Save**, as shown in Figure 2.4.

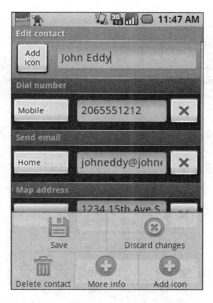

Figure 2.4
Pressing the Menu button offers several options for actions you can perform for the current record.

You'll notice that when you press the Menu button, you have a few other options, as shown in Figure 2.4:

- **Discard changes:** This simply undoes all the changes you just made. Any information that was previously saved in the contact is preserved.

- **Delete contact:** This does exactly what you'd expect—it deletes the contact.

- **More info:** This option performs exactly like the More info button within the contact itself.

- **Add icon:** This option also performs exactly like the Add icon button within the contact. It allows you to specify an icon for the contact.

Now that you have a bunch of information on your contact, we can look at doing something with that contact.

Calling a Contact

Because this is a mobile phone, let's start with calling a contact. Follow these steps:

1. Press the **Home** button to return to the Home screen.

2. Access the dialer by either tapping the **Dialer** icon on the screen, pressing the green **Send** button, or opening the Dialer from the **Application** tab.

3. Tap the **Contacts** tab.

4. Tap the contact you want to call.

5. If you have multiple phone numbers for the contact, tap the phone number you'd like to call.

You can also tap and hold a particular contact record to bring up a menu that allows you to call the contact immediately. Only the default phone number (which is the Mobile number unless you have specified otherwise) is available from this quick launch menu.

There's another way to dial a contact that's fun and easy, especially if you're using a hands-free car kit with your phone. Hold down the green Send button to display the Voice Dialer application, as shown in Figure 2.5. It lists a few examples of what you can say to call specific contacts.

Figure 2.5
Voice dialing allows you nearly hands-free operation.

Sending a Contact a Text Message

Hopefully you read all about sending text messages in Chapter 1, "The Phone Basics." Now that you have some contacts entered, we'll explore sending text messages by selecting a contact rather than by entering a phone number.

➔   For more information about sending text messages, **see** "Text Messaging," **p. 21**.

There are several ways to send a text message to a contact. We'll start with the original method:

1.   Tap the **Application** tab, tap **Messaging**, and then tap **New message**.

2.   With the keyboard, start typing the name of one of your contacts. As shown in Figure 2.6, your phone tries to complete your typing with the name of one or more of your contacts.

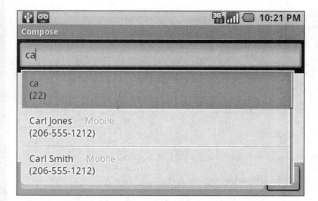

Figure 2.6
Type the name of one of your contacts.

If you have multiple contacts with similar first names, you might get a choice when you start typing the name. For example, if you have a contact named John Eddy and another named Joan Eddy, typing Jo produces a pop-up box with both of those names listed. Just tap the specific contact you want.

The previous method isn't the only way you can send a text message to a contact, however. You can follow these steps to send a text message directly from the Contacts list:

1.   Tap the **Application** tab, and then tap **Contacts**.

2.   Tap and hold one of your contacts until you see the pop-up menu.

3.   Tap **Send SMS/MMS**.

4.   Type your message, and tap **Send**.

If you don't see Send SMS/MMS on the pop-up menu, you probably tried to send a message to a contact who doesn't have a phone number entered.

But wait—there's more! There is one last way to send a text message to a contact. It is particularly helpful if the contact has more than one phone number:

1. Tap the **Application** tab, and then tap **Contacts**.

2. Select one of your contacts to open his or her record.

3. Under **Send SMS/MMS**, tap the phone number that you want to use to send a text message.

4. Type your message, and tap **Send**.

Mapping a Contact's Address

After you've added a postal address for a contact, you can see where that address is located in Google Maps by following these steps:

1. Tap the **Application** tab, and then tap **Contacts**.

2. Tap a contact who has a postal address.

3. Scroll down to **Map address**, and tap the address you'd like to map.

4. Your contact's address is mapped, as shown in Figure 2.7.

Figure 2.7
You can map any address you've entered for a contact.

Setting Up Favorite Contacts

We all have good friends. And then we have favorite friends—those we want to be able to find more easily or contact all the time.

Did you notice the Favorites tab at the top of the Dialer screen? The following steps show you how to add a contact to your Favorites:

1. Tap the **Application** tab, and tap **Contacts**.

2. Tap and hold one of your contacts.

3. When the pop-up menu appears, tap **Add to Favorites**.

Now, whenever you need to find one of your favorite contacts, just open the Dialer and tap Favorites.

Transferring Contacts from Another Phone

The instructions in this section refer to phones that use a SIM card. Not all mobile phones and mobile phone companies use SIM cards. If your old mobile phone or your new Android-powered phone don't support SIM cards, you need to contact your mobile phone provider for specific instructions on transferring contacts.

If you happen to have contacts stored on another phone, you'll first want to look into the instructions for your old phone for how to move the contacts to your SIM card. After you've moved the contacts to the SIM card, just follow these steps to pull the contacts on the SIM into the Contacts program on your Android-powered phone:

1. Tap the **Application** tab, and then tap **Contacts**.

2. Press the **Menu** button.

3. Tap **Settings**.

4. Tap **SIM contacts importer** to display the screen shown in Figure 2.8.

5. Tap a contact one at a time, or press the **Menu** button and touch **Import all**.

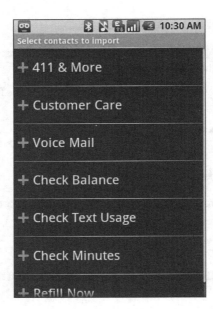

Figure 2.8
Tap to import your contacts one at a time.

Transferring Contacts from Your Computer

Unfortunately, there isn't a way to transfer contacts directly to your phone from your computer. However, you *can* import them into Gmail. Gmail imports your contacts from a comma-separated value file that most programs, such as Outlook, Outlook Express, Yahoo!, and Hotmail, can produce. For specific instructions on exporting your contacts from these programs, consult the Help files for those programs.

After your contacts are in Gmail, they can be synced to your phone.

Deleting a Contact

Maybe you broke up. Maybe you had a fight. Maybe you just want to delete the test contact you created earlier in the chapter. Whatever your reason for deleting a contact, the following steps show you how to permanently remove a contact from your phone:

1. Tap the **Application** tab, and then tap **Contacts**.

2. Tap and hold the contact you'd like to delete, and touch **Delete** on the pop-up menu.

3. Tap **OK** to permanently delete the contact.

You can also delete a contact by opening the contact, pressing the Menu button, and tapping Delete contact. You still need to tap OK to confirm the deletion.

What About All That Other Stuff?

Although we've shown you around the various menus available on the phone, you might have noticed a few things we didn't talk about yet.

To be honest, there are so many interlinked, cross-referenced, related features in this phone, it's extraordinarily hard not to put the cart before the horse. Don't worry; we will talk about those other features in the following chapters.

Using Your Calendar

You're busy, you're on the go, you have a hectic social schedule and a manic Monday at work, week after week. You need a program that will help you keep track of your where-to-goes and what-to-dos—something like a calendar. Google is wonderful enough to provide you with one, both on the phone and on the Internet. Changes you make to the calendar on the phone are automatically synchronized with your computer, and changes you make on your computer are automatically synchronized with the phone. It's almost like magic!

Most of what we'll talk about in this chapter centers around what you can do on your phone. However, we'll also touch on a few things that you can only access on your computer. After you've configured some of the calendaring features on your computer, you can access them on your phone as well.

Viewing Your Calendar

Even if you haven't used your calendar at http://calendar.google.com yet, all you need to do to see your calendar is open the Application tab and tap the Calendar icon. You should see something like Figure 3.1.

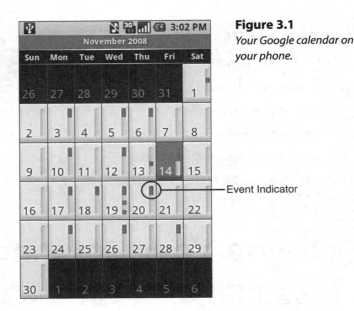

Figure 3.1
Your Google calendar on your phone.

Event Indicator

When you first open your calendar, you are likely looking at the default Monthly view. If your calendar doesn't look like the figure, press the Menu button, and tap Month to switch your view.

At the top of the screen, you see the current month and year. Any day that has an event has a green bar to the right of the date number.

If you want to scroll backward and forward through days of the week or months, simply drag your finger up and down the screen.

Monthly view is the best view for seeing what day of the week November 11 is, and to see if you're generally free next Wednesday, but it isn't all that helpful for seeing your schedule for a particular day. There are multiple ways to do this:

- Tap the day you want to see.

- Tap and hold a particular day. When the pop-up box appears, tap Day to get the screen in Figure 3.2.

- Press the Menu button, and tap Day. This opens the daily calendar for the currently selected day.

While you're in Daily view, you can drag your finger up and down the screen to scroll through the day, and left and right to move to a previous or later day.

If you want to see the whole week, press the Menu button and tap Week. This shows you the weekly schedule for whatever week you just selected.

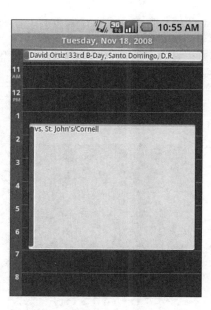

Figure 3.2
Choose Day from the pop-up menu to open a day.

As in Day view, scrolling up and down moves you through the day of the week, and left and right moves you to earlier and later weeks.

Has playing around with the navigation caused you to get lost in a different day, week, or month? Just press the Menu button and tap Today.

Viewing Other Calendars

One of the great features of Google Calendar is the ability to add other people's calendars to your own, viewing their schedules alongside yours. This doesn't work for just your friends' calendars, but for public calendars too! You can easily add holidays, both national and foreign, sports schedules, and even DVD release dates. You can't add public calendars directly from your phone, so we'll cover that a little later in this chapter, in the section "Some Tasks You Can't Perform from the Phone."

To add a calendar, follow these steps:

1. While in the Calendar, press the **Menu** button.
2. Tap **More**.
3. Tap **My calendars**.
4. Tap to select the calendars you want to view.

You'll note that each calendar has a different color next to it. This is shown in Figure 3.3, although it's hard to see in black and white. When you're looking at your calendar, that color appears next to each appointment to indicate which calendar it is from.

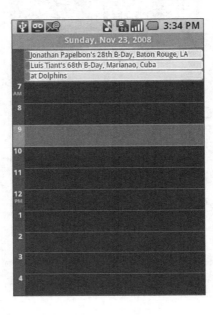

Figure 3.3
You can display appointments from multiple calendars at once.

Creating a New Appointment

She said "Yes" to a movie! He said "Sure" to dinner! You have a doctor's appointment! Your buddy called, and he has tickets to the big game! Whatever the reason, eventually you'll need to create an appointment.

Of course, there are a few different ways to do so:

- From the Calendar, press the Menu button, and tap New event.

- In Daily view, tap and hold the time that you want your appointment to start. Then tap New event on the pop-up menu.

- In Weekly view, tap and hold the day and time that you want your appointment to start. Then tap New event on the pop-up menu.

- In Monthly view, tap and hold the day on which you want your appointment to be. Then tap New event on the pop-up menu.

No matter which method you use, you end up with an Event details form. It should look something like Figure 3.4.

Figure 3.4
Create a new event.

Because forgetting a friend or relative's birthday always leads to hurt feelings, we'll go through the following steps to create a new appointment for a birthday:

1. Using any of the previously listed methods, create a new, empty event.

2. In the **What** field, enter the subject—in this case, **John's Birthday**.

3. In the **From** field, tap the date, and change the month, day, and year to whatever is appropriate for your event. You can use the plus and minus buttons to shift the date a few days in either direction, or type the date directly.

4. If this is an all-day event, tap the **All day** check box to select it.

5. Tap the **Where** field, and enter a location.

6. Tap the **Description** field, and enter a longer description if necessary.

7. If you have multiple calendars, tap the **Calendar** drop-down list, and select the calendar that you want to use for your event. You can choose only one calendar.

8. Tap the **Reminder** field, and choose a date for the event reminder. Tap **X** if you don't want a reminder.

9. Tap the **Repeats** field, and choose a recurrence pattern. For a birthday, for example, drag your finger up the screen, and then tap **Yearly** to select it.

10. Press the **Menu** button, and tap **Show extra options**. The next two options are not required, but we'll list them here just in case you find them useful.

11. Tap the **Presence** drop-down to change the presence information. Presence allows you to define a block of time as free or busy. So if others share your calendar, they know if you are available during a certain block of time.

12. Tap the **Privacy** drop-down to choose whether your event is private or public. A private event appears as busy on your calendar, but no details are available to those viewing your calendar.

13. Tap **Save** to save your event.

You might have noticed an Add reminder option when pressing the Menu button and wondered why that option is there when you just added a reminder. Well, an appointment can have more than one reminder. In fact, it can have as many as five different reminders.

Viewing Your Agenda

You might have noticed the Agenda option as you were changing views here and there. The Agenda view is an easy way to see all the events for a month in one simple list. It's really most useful after you've added a few events to your calendar. Otherwise, you're just looking at a boring screen with little to no information instead of something exciting, such as Figure 3.5.

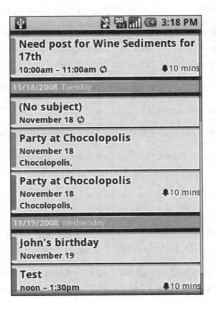

Figure 3.5
The Agenda view shows all your events for the current month.

If a day doesn't have an event, it isn't listed in the Agenda view.

You can access the Agenda view using two different methods:

- From any calendar view, press the Menu button, and tap Agenda.
- From the weekly or monthly view, tap and hold anywhere on the screen, and then tap Agenda.

Whatever month you happen to be viewing will be the month pulled up in the Agenda view.

We have one last little bit of information about the Agenda view. If you are viewing the agenda for the current month, pressing the Menu button and tapping Today scrolls the Agenda so that today is at the top of the screen. If you're viewing a different month, the Today option currently doesn't work.

Reminder Settings and Other Options

You can configure a variety of options for your calendar, including default reminder settings and default view settings. Configuring default reminder settings causes the same type of reminder to be played for every event. You can always change the reminder setting for a specific event when you create that event.

To access these other options, press the Menu button, tap More, and then tap Settings.

You can also access these settings from the keyboard by pressing the Menu button and P key simultaneously.

The Calendar view setting allows you to hide events that you've been invited to but have declined. Tap the check box to select it.

The Reminder settings section has a variety of options.

Set Alerts & Notifications

Tap Set alerts & notifications to control how the reminder is displayed. You can choose from the following options:

- **Alert:** This option displays a pop-up window when the reminder occurs, as shown in Figure 3.6.

- **Status bar notification:** This is the default option and places an alert in the status bar when the reminder occurs, as shown in Figure 3.7.

- **Off:** This turns off all notifications of your reminder, which is much the same as not having a reminder at all. Selecting this option turns off a few other options such as Select ringtone and Vibrate.

Reminder Notification

Figure 3.6
A reminder pops up on the screen.

Figure 3.7
The status bar displays a small reminder notification.

Select Ringtone

Tap Select ringtone to choose the ringtone you want played when your reminder occurs. As shown in Figure 3.8, you can choose from a variety of ringtones that you have on your phone. Tap the specific ringtone you want played when your reminder occurs, and then tap OK to save your changes.

Vibrate

Tap this option to enable or disable vibration. You can have your reminder play a ringtone, vibrate, or both play a ringtone and vibrate.

Figure 3.8
Choose a ringtone for your reminder.

Set Default Reminder

Tap the Set default reminder option to configure the timing of your default reminder, as shown in Figure 3.9. You can choose from a variety of time settings. For example, if you tap 12 hours, your reminder will occur 12 hours before the start time of your event.

Figure 3.9
Choose a default reminder time.

Some Tasks You Can't Perform from the Phone

If you've used a calendar at work, you're probably wondering how you can use your phone to invite people to a meeting, create a new calendar, share a calendar, or access a public calendar. Unfortunately, you can't do any of these tasks directly from your phone, but you can do them from your computer and access some of the functionality from your phone.

Creating a Second Calendar

Let's start with creating a second calendar, which is a pretty common thing to want to do. Here are the steps:

1. On your computer, open a Web browser and go to http://calendar.google.com. Make sure you're signed in with the same account that your phone is configured to use.

2. On the left side of the screen, in the My calendars section, click **Create** to open the Create New Calendar form, shown in Figure 3.10.

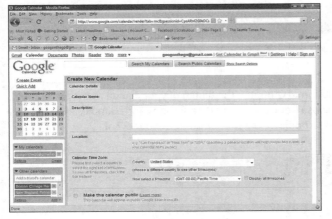

Figure 3.10
You can create multiple calendars.

3. Enter the appropriate information in the **Calendar Name**, **Description**, **Location**, and **Calendar Time Zone** fields.

4. Leave **Make this calendar public** unchecked.

5. If you want to share this calendar with others, enter their email addresses in the **Share with specific people** field.

6. Click **Create Calendar**.

Making your calendar public allows anyone to see it. This might be great, for example, if you're in a garage band and you want people to be able to find your gigs. It's probably not such a good idea if you're creating a business calendar.

After you've created a calendar on your computer, you can access it on your phone.

→   For more information on accessing multiple calendars, **see** "Viewing Other Calendars," p. 45.

Sharing an Existing Calendar

Another task you can accomplish on your computer is sharing your calendar with other people. We talked about that briefly when we created a new calendar, but you also can open an existing calendar and share that with others. Click Settings in the My calendars section of your Google Calendar to display the view shown in Figure 3.11.

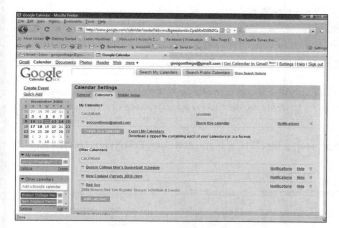

Figure 3.11

Access a variety of calendar settings.

To share your calendar, click the Share this calendar link next to whichever of your calendars you want to share. Enter the email addresses of anyone you want to share with, and then click Save.

Adding a Public Calendar

From the main Google Calendar page on your computer, there's a section for Other calendars. Click Add, and then choose Add a public calendar. As shown in Figure 3.12, you can choose from a variety of popular calendars, click a category of calendars, or search for a public calendar, such as that of your favorite sports team.

As soon as you've found the calendar you want, click the Add to Calendar button. All the events on that calendar are added to your calendar.

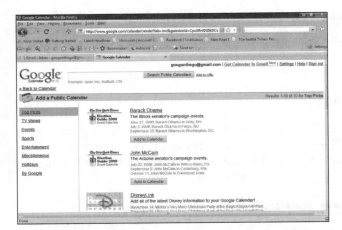

Figure 3.12
There are many categories of public calendars.

Inviting People to a Meeting

One last thing that we'd like to talk about that can be done only through the Web interface is inviting guests to events. If you want to invite a guest to an appointment or event, follow these steps:

1. Open the event on your computer by clicking it and selecting **Edit Event Details** (see Figure 3.13).

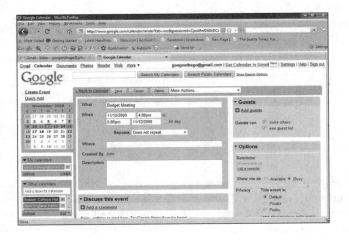

Figure 3.13
Invite guests to your events.

2. Click **Add guests**.

3. Enter the email addresses of your guests, separated by commas.

4. Click **Save** to send the invitations to your guests.

Unfortunately, currently there's no way to do any of this from your phone, but these features might be added over time.

4

Working with Email

Overview of Gmail

One of the key reasons to pick up one of the Android-powered phones is how closely hooked into your Google accounts they are—the calendar, the contacts, the maps. But right now we'll talk about Google's second-biggest killer application—Gmail.

On the surface, it's just another Web-based email client. But something about it draws people in. Perhaps it's the large amount of storage that Gmail makes available to users for free. Or perhaps it was the invitation-only scheme they used for years that gave it an air of exclusivity. Whatever the reason, Gmail remains one of the most popular Web-based mail clients.

It uses a relatively unique method of displaying messages, grouping them by threads, so that as you exchange emails, they take up only one line in your inbox.

Reading Email

Reading email is quick and easy. Whenever you receive a new email, you get a nice little notification on the status bar to let you know, as shown in Figure 4.1.

Email Notification

Figure 4.1
The Status bar shows your email notification.

Now, just like every other time you get a status bar notification in the upper left, you can tap the status bar and drag it down the screen to see your notifications. Note that, as shown in Figure 4.2, you can just tap Clear notifications to get rid of all the notifications, or you can tap the notification in question to pull up—well, whatever the notification is for. In the case of email, you just tap New email. Because, as we said, Gmail stores emails as conversations, you see some number of unread conversations. If it's only one, tapping the New email notification loads that one unread email. If you have multiple unread conversations, you instead end up in your Inbox.

"Wait a minute," I hear you saying. "What about reading all the mail in my Inbox that isn't new? How do I get there?" That's easy enough. Just open the Application tab and tap Gmail (see Figure 4.3).

You can use the trackball or your finger to scroll through the list. If a conversation has an unread message, it's bold in the list, with a white background.

Tap an email to open it. If it's a completely read conversation, you see the most recent message, along with a link to tap to see all the messages. If the conversation contains unread messages, they are all open for you to read.

Figure 4.2
Clearing all your notifications at once.

Figure 4.3
The Gmail icon in all its resplendent glory.

The Gmail Icon

If you receive a message with an attachment, you can preview most Microsoft Office file types and images by tapping the Preview button. You can also save some attachment types, such as pictures and graphics, by tapping the Download button, as shown in Figure 4.4.

Figure 4.4
You can preview or download attachments.

Whenever you read email, you can press the Back button to get back to your Inbox. Or you can press the Menu button and then tap More and Back to Inbox.

The menu has a few other options besides the More button, as shown in Figure 4.5:

- **Archive:** Archiving an email removes it from your Inbox without actually deleting it. We'll talk about the difference later.

- **Add star:** Stars are just one way to organize your mailbox by adding an icon to emails that you want to flag for some reason.

- **Mark unread:** Marks the email, or the conversation, as unread.

- **Change labels:** This allows you to set one or more labels on a message. Labels will appear at the top of the message/conversation.

- **Delete:** Delete actually deletes a message or conversation.

- **More:** Gives you access to Back to Inbox, which we just mentioned, and Report spam, which is used to let Google know that a spam message sneaked through the Google spam filters. This option removes the spam from your Inbox and helps improve Google's spam filters.

If you press the Menu button again and scroll to the bottom of the message, you'll find six more buttons. The first three are visible for every message in a conversation, and the last three are at the bottom of the conversation.

Figure 4.5
The Menu button is always useful.

- **Reply:** This starts a new message in the conversation to the person who sent the message you're currently reading.

- **Reply to all:** This starts a new message in the conversation to all the people on the To or Cc line of the message you're currently reading.

- **Forward:** This starts a new message and requires you to provide the address of whomever you want to forward an existing message to.

- **Archive:** Archiving a conversation removes it from your Inbox. The conversation is stored in the All Mail folder.

- **Labels:** You can add and remove labels for the conversation. A label is an easy way to categorize a message or conversation.

- **Delete:** This is just another way to delete the conversation.

As you can see, the buttons on the email and conversation are pretty self-explanatory, so we'll go back to the Inbox and take a look at the other options you have there.

Now that you're in the Inbox, press the Menu button to examine the following options:

- **Refresh:** Although your phone should regularly update your list of messages for you on-the-fly, if it hasn't, you can tap this option to refresh the list.

- **Compose:** When you want to create a new message, this is what you tap. We'll cover this more a little later in this chapter.

- **View labels:** You tap this option when you want to view the labels you have given to messages.

- **Search:** This is what Google is known for—searching for stuff or, in this case, your email. Tap this option, type in what you want to search for, and off you go.

- **Settings:** Tap this option to view your email settings. We'll cover this option in the section "Customizing Gmail Settings."

Sending a New Message

Even though reading email is fun and exciting, at some point you'll want to send email as well. To send a new message, follow these steps:

1. From your Inbox, press the **Menu** button.

2. Tap **Compose** to bring up the form shown in Figure 4.6.

Figure 4.6
The new message form.

3. Type an address in the **To** box. If the recipient is in your Contacts, the phone automatically fills in the email address as you type. This process is known as autocomplete.

4. Tap in the **Subject** box, and type a subject.

5. Scroll down to the large, unmarked field and tap to start typing the body of your email.

6. Tap **Send** when you're done to send your message.

While you're composing a new message, you can access several options by pressing the Menu button:

- **Send:** This is just another way to send your message.

- **Add Cc/Bcc:** This adds the Cc and Bcc fields so that you can add recipients to those fields.

- **Attach:** If you have a picture stored on the phone, you can attach it to the message and send it.

- **Edit subject:** This option is helpful if you are replying to an existing message or forwarding an existing message. Tap this to change the subject.

- **Discard:** This sends the message to the trash immediately. Be careful with this option, because you receive no warning message.

Replying to or Forwarding a Message

These tasks are so easy, they don't even need steps. Simply open the message you want to reply to or forward. Tap a button at the bottom of the message to either Reply, Reply to all, or Forward the message. These actions do the following:

- **Reply:** This creates a new message to the person who sent you the original message.

- **Reply to all:** This creates a new message to the person who sent you the original message and anyone else who received the message because their name was on the To or Cc line.

- **Forward:** This sends the existing message to another person. You can also add a comment to the message before you send it.

Archiving an Email

We mentioned both archiving and deleting. Both actions remove an email from your Inbox. However, that's where the similarities end. Unlike most other email clients, Gmail doesn't have folders, so to speak. Figure 4.7 shows a typical Gmail account.

Folder Structure

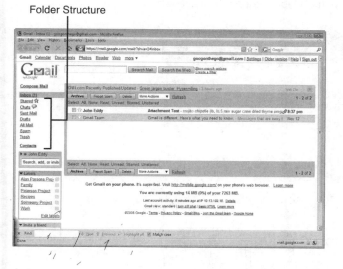

Figure 4.7
A typical Gmail account.

The Inbox is where all received mail goes automatically, unless it has been marked as spam. The Inbox stores all mail that hasn't been trashed, marked as spam, or archived.

The All Mail folder is all email messages that haven't been marked as spam or trashed. So it includes any mail that has been archived. It also includes all messages you've sent, as well as all messages that are currently in draft form.

The Trash folder stores all mail that you've deleted. When you delete (or trash) a message, it is stored in the Trash folder for 30 days. On the 31st day, it's deleted forever. If there's any chance that you might need a message later, do not send it to the trash. This is a bit like storing your tax returns or your driver's license in the garbage.

So what is the Archive? Archiving an email simply removes it from the Inbox. If you like the peace of mind of looking at a clean, organized Inbox with just a few items, you'll probably archive items often. However, because Gmail offers you such a great amount of storage, there is no real reason to archive other than organization. Archived items can still be found in the All Mail folder.

All About Labels

Because Google stores all the unarchived mail in one giant Inbox, as soon as you get more than a handful of messages, you'll probably sometimes need to search your Inbox for specific messages. Although this works quite well most of the time, sometimes it's more convenient to set aside certain messages for easy retrieval.

That's one of the primary functions of labels. They help you organize your mail within your Inbox or within the All Mail folder. While you're viewing a message, press the Menu button, and then tap View Labels to display the screen shown in Figure 4.8. Just tap the label you want to apply. You can apply multiple labels to a single message.

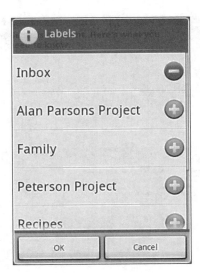

Figure 4.8
You can tap any of the labels you have defined.

You can also add labels by tapping and holding a single message and choosing Change labels from the pop-up menu.

Although applying labels is quite easy, there is no way to create new labels on your phone. To do that, you need to open www.gmail.com on your computer and sign in with the same account you're using on your phone. From there, you can edit labels or create new ones.

Applying Labels to Received Mail Automatically

Although it's useful to be able to apply labels to mail you have received, it isn't very efficient. The following steps show you how you can automatically apply labels to new messages as you receive them:

1. On your computer, open Gmail and click the **Edit labels** option on the left side of the screen.

2. Click the word **Filters** at the top of the screen.

3. Click **Create a new filter**.

Although we're showing you only a small feature of filters, perhaps we should mention what filters are. Essentially, filters are what you would call rules in most other mail programs, a way to do things to messages automatically. In this case, we're going to be automatically applying a label to messages as they come in so that you can more easily find them on your phone.

4. Specify the criteria you want, such as **From:** john@doe.com or **Has the words:** "Family Reunion."

5. Click **Test Search** to verify that the filter captures the messages you intend. If not, continue editing the criteria.

6. Click **Next Step** and choose the action you want to happen when you receive a filtered message. You can take a variety of actions, including applying a label.

7. Choose the label you'd like to apply, and then click **Create Filter**.

Within Gmail, you can see only email that has this label, giving your Inbox the appearance of folders without actually having them. You might think that sounds rather silly, and that folders are far more convenient, but consider this: Unless you make a copy, thus doubling the size of the message, it can't exist in two folders. But you can put as many labels as you want on a message. So, that work-related email about the Peterson Project? You can use the "Work" label, the "Peterson Project" label, and the "From Dave" label, thus making this message easy to find in all three filtered views.

How's that for efficiency?

Customizing Gmail Settings

Let's go back to the Inbox on the phone. Press the Menu button and tap Settings. You can configure two types of options: General settings and Notification settings.

General Settings

In the General settings section, you have the following options:

- **Signature:** A signature is a blurb of text that appears at the bottom of your email messages. You can use only text. Images are not supported. The signature you specify here is specific to your phone, so you can set up something to show that you're typing on a tiny keyboard and might make some typographic errors. Or you can brag about your new phone. For example, I set up the following signature on my phone: I'm mailing you from my spiffy new G1 Google Phone, but the keyboard is rather small, so please excuse any errors.

- **Labels:** As we just showed you, labels are a powerful little feature. Perhaps you want to receive only certain emails on your phone, and you've set up a filter to automatically apply a certain label to emails. Here you can select synchronization settings for any label, as shown in Figure 4.9. This will affect what messages get downloaded to your phone, which can be very useful if you happen to have a data plan that limits the amount of data you are able to download. Currently, for your Inbox, you have two options: Sync recent or Sync all, while all other labels have a third option of blank. Honestly, between you, me and the untold others reading this book, this feature as it is while I'm writing isn't very useful. If you were able to set the Inbox not to synchronize, but synchronize only starred items or certain labels, then it would be far more useful. But, as it stands, you can't not sync the Inbox, so to only sync certain items, you'd need to set up a filter that archives everything that you don't want to get on your phone. Which would then make the web-based interface mostly useless. The key reason to use this feature is to sync all items for a particular label, so you'll always be able to see them.

To change the settings for each label, just tap the label. You can choose from the following options:

- **Sync all:** This option simply means that all items with this label will be synchronized with your phone.

- **Sync recent:** This option synchronizes all unread items.

- **Blank:** If the synchronization has no option listed, none of the items will be synchronized.

Figure 4.9
Configuring synchronization settings for your phone.

Notification Settings

You can configure several different notification options, as shown in Figure 4.10.

Figure 4.10
Configuring notification options for your phone.

- **Email notifications:** By default, your phone notifies you with an icon in the status bar every time you get a new message. Tap this option to deselect it if you don't want this to happen.

- **Select ringtone:** Tap this option to choose a ringtone to play whenever you get a new message.

- **Vibrate:** If this option is checked, your phone vibrates whenever you get a new message.

Connecting to Other Email Accounts

Gmail is a great application, but lots of people have other email accounts. You'll be glad to know that you can hook up to any POP3/IMAP4 mail server. Although some Web-based mail providers have POP3/IMAP4 access options, not all of them do. Others have the option but require you to pay extra for it or use only approved email clients. Be sure to check with your mail provider if you aren't sure or if the steps provided don't seem to work for you. The setup is quick and easy, and you can add several other email accounts with ease, as shown in the following steps.

You might be wondering what the difference is between POP3 and IMAP4. There are a number of differences, but the one you will probably care about the most is that POP3 is designed to retrieve email from your Inbox. IMAP4 is designed to interact with your Inbox and other folders. So, if you mark a message as read in an IMAP folder, both the server and the client see that the message is read. Two-way communication occurs between the client (the phone) and the server. If you have a POP3 account, your phone can retrieve messages from the server, but it cannot change the message's read or unread state.

1. Tap the **Application** tab, and then tap **Email**.

2. If this is your first non-Google email account, tap **Next** and skip to step 5. Otherwise, press the **Menu** button, and then tap **Accounts**.

3. Enter the email address and password for your account. Tap **Next**.

4. Your phone attempts to retrieve the settings for your email account. If this fails (it often does, because not all servers support downloading these settings automatically), continue with the next step. Otherwise, skip to step 8.

5. Tap the button for the account type you want to add.

6. Enter your incoming mail server settings. You need to obtain these from your email provider.

7. Tap **Next**. Your phone validates your incoming email settings.

8. Enter your outgoing server settings, as shown in Figure 4.11, and tap **Next**.

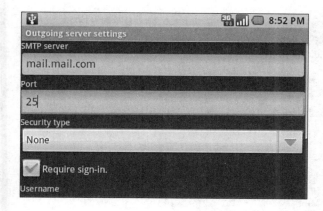

Figure 4.11

Entering the outgoing server settings for your account.

9. When your account is validated, you're asked for some basic information, such as how often you'd like your phone to check for email and whether you want to be notified when you receive new messages. Tap **Next** when you're done.

10. Enter a name for your account if you'd like. You don't need to enter a name, but it can be helpful if you have multiple accounts.

11. Enter your name. This is the name that is displayed whenever someone else reads your email. Tap **Save**, and you're done.

When setting up a POP3 account, you need to set one option carefully. POP3 clients normally remove messages from the server after they are downloaded. The phone, however, does not. If you want, you can configure the phone to delete messages from the server when you delete them from your Inbox or after seven days.

You can now send and receive email messages on your phone. You can create multiple accounts from different providers.

Reading Email

We don't need to say much about reading email. From the Home screen, tap the Application tab, and then tap Email. Tap the email account you want (if you have more than one), and then tap Inbox. Tap any of the existing messages to open and read them.

If your email came with an attachment, scroll to the bottom of the message to see it. Figure 4.12 shows a message with several attachments.

Figure 4.12
Each message can have multiple attachments.

Your phone can't download or view every attachment type, but if the attachment is one you can work with, you see an Open or Save button, or both. Tap the button to perform the action.

Sending a New Message

Sending a new email is almost as easy as reading one. From the email account, press the Menu button, and tap Compose. From there, just follow the same instructions that you used for Gmail.

Press the Menu button to display the following options:

- **Add Cc/Bcc:** As before, this option lets you add Cc and Bcc fields to the message.
- **Send:** This sends the message.
- **Save as draft:** This saves the message locally on the phone in case you want to finish it later.
- **Discard:** Be careful with this option. If you tap it, the message is deleted immediately.
- **Add attachment:** Tap this option to attach a picture to the email.

→ For more information about adding pictures to an email message, **see** "Sharing by Email," **p. 74**.

Replying to or Forwarding a Message

Replying to a message is easy. Either open the message and tap the Reply/Reply all/Forward button at the bottom of the message, or tap and hold the message and tap Reply, Reply all, or Forward, depending on what you want to do.

Deleting a Message

If you're reading the message, just scroll to the bottom and tap the Delete button to delete it. If you're looking at your message list, tap and hold the email you'd like to delete, and then tap Delete.

Switching Between Multiple Accounts

Assuming that you have multiple POP3/IMAP accounts defined, simply follow these steps to switch between them:

1. Tap the **Application** tab, and then tap **Email**.
2. Press the **Menu** button.
3. Tap **Accounts**.
4. Tap the account you want to use.

Removing an Account

If you are ready to get rid of one of your POP3/IMAP4 accounts, doing so is quite easy:

1. Tap the **Application** tab, and then tap **Email**.
2. Press the **Menu** button.
3. Tap **Accounts**.
4. In your list of accounts, tap and hold the account you'd like to take off your phone.
5. Tap **Remove account**. If you're sure, tap **OK**.

Taking Pictures

With the exception of some business-related phones, most phones available these days have a camera built into them. Although it might not be as good as the pocket-sized camera you take on vacations, most are easily as good as the cameras that were available for several hundred dollars just four or five years ago. Having a camera that's always with you can be very helpful. You can take a picture of a car accident that you've just been in, or shop for appliances or carpet and send images back home. This chapter walks you through using your camera, as well as a number of things you can do with the pictures you take.

Taking Pictures with Your Phone

When people purchase a mobile phone, the first three things they usually do are make a phone call, change the ringtone (or at least listen to a number of them), and take a picture. If you want to use your phone to take a picture, follow these steps:

1. Tap the **Application** tab, and then tap **Camera**.

2. Aim the camera at the target.

3. Press the trackball to capture the image. The camera might try to focus the image first, so keep the phone steady until you see the captured image on the screen.

Most mobile phones also have a button somewhere on the phone that can be used to launch the camera. On the G1, it is on the lower-right side of the phone. Hold down the button for about 4 seconds, or until the camera application launches.

After the phone captures the image, you see the options shown in Figure 5.1.

Figure 5.1
You can perform several different actions with your photo.

Save

This option saves the picture to your phone. Most mobile phones have enough storage for hundreds of pictures.

Set As

This set of options allows you to associate the photo with a contact or save it as the phone's wallpaper.

Saving a Picture with a Contact

Saving a picture with a contact does two things.

- When you open the contact, you see his or her picture at the top of the screen, as shown in Figure 5.2.

- When you receive a call from the contact, you see his or her picture on the screen.

Only one picture at a time can be associated with a contact.

Figure 5.2
You see a photo of your contact.

To save a picture with a contact, follow these steps:

1. From the picture, tap **Set as**.

2. Tap **Contact**.

3. Select your contact from the list of contacts.

4. Drag the small box that appears around the picture to select the portion of the image that you want to use for your contact. You might not be able to select the entire picture, depending on how big it is, so drag the box to highlight the part of the picture you want to see.

5. Tap **Save** when you're happy with the photo, or tap **Discard** if you want to start over.

Setting a Picture as Your Wallpaper

The second option you have after you tap Set is to save the picture as your phone's wallpaper. You know that watery vista that appears on your phone when you're looking at the home screen? That's your phone's wallpaper. You can change this wallpaper to anything you'd like.

To save a picture as the phone's wallpaper, follow these steps:

1. From the picture, tap **Set as**.

2. Tap **Wallpaper**.

3. Drag the rectangular box that appears around your picture. You might not be able to select the entire picture.

4. Tap **Save** when you're happy with the photo, or tap **Discard** if you want to start over.

Your phone's home screen should now look a little different, as shown in Figure 5.3. Now sure, this picture isn't a pretty sunset or our cat or dog; it's just a picture I took while my co-author (and husband) was driving me around in our convertible. And the joy of setting your wallpaper is being able to select whatever you want, be it a random picture of your husband, or a picture of Rover, or even the sunset at Waikiki.

Figure 5.3
You can change your phone's wallpaper.

Share

This set of options allows you to send your picture to other people. You can choose from the following sharing options:

- **Email:** If you have set up a POP3 or IMAP4 account, you can send the picture through the default account.

- **Google mail:** Choosing this option creates a new Gmail message and automatically attaches the image.

- **Messaging:** This option lets you send the picture as a Multimedia Message System message. This is very much like a text message.

Sharing by Email

To share a picture by email or Google mail, follow these steps:

1. With the picture to be shared in view, tap **Share**.

2. Tap **Email** to display the screen shown in Figure 5.4.

Figure 5.4
Sharing your picture with other people.

3.   If you chose **Email** and you have multiple email accounts, tap the account you want to use. Otherwise, proceed with step 4.

4.   Enter the recipient's address in the **To** field.

5.   Enter a subject.

6.   Enter a message.

7.   Tap **Send**.

→   For more information about using email on your phone, **see** "Sending a New Message," **p. 60**.

Sharing Photos by Messaging

Sharing a picture by messaging sends what is known as a Multimedia Message System (MMS) message. An MMS message is a lot like a text message, although not all phones can receive MMS messages. If you are sending someone an MMS message, first you should verify that he or she can receive MMS messages. In addition, your recipient will likely be charged for each MMS message he or she receives, and you will be charged for each one you send.

To share your picture in an MMS message, follow these steps:

1.   With the picture to be shared in view, tap **Share**.

2.   Tap **Messaging**.

3.   If your picture is too large, the phone asks you to resize the image before sending. Tap **Resize** to compress the image.

4.   Enter the recipient's phone number in the **To** field.

5.   Use the keyboard to enter a message.

6.   Tap **Send**.

If you want to cancel an MMS message, there's only one way to do it on the G1. Press the Back button on the phone. You're asked if you want to discard the message. Tap OK to discard, or tap Cancel if you pressed this button by mistake.

Delete

This option is fairly obvious. There is no warning after you tap Delete. The picture is immediately and permanently deleted.

Camera Settings

When the camera is active, you can press the Menu button to configure a few basic settings. Tap Settings to display the screen shown in Figure 5.5. You have two options:

- **Store location in pictures:** If you select this item, latitude and longitude data is stored along with your picture. The data is collected from the phone's location when the picture was taken.

- **Prompt after capture:** Remember all those options you get after taking a picture? You can disable all of them by tapping to uncheck Prompt after capture. If you disable the automatic prompts, you can always view those options again by pressing the Menu button after you've taken a picture.

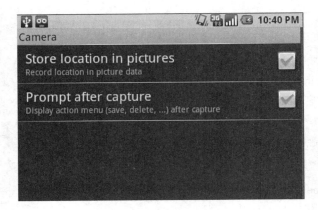

Figure 5.5
You can change camera settings, such as the location.

Viewing Pictures You've Taken

Now that you've probably taken a lot of pictures of your house or cat or best friend, you're probably wondering how to access them. You have two methods:

- From the home screen, tap the Application tab, and tap Pictures.

- Activate the camera, press the Menu button, and tap Pictures.

Either method brings you to a screen that looks something like Figure 5.6 or Figure 5.7.

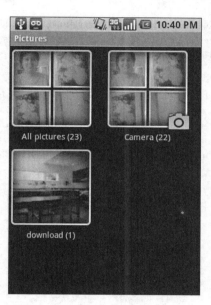

Figure 5.6
Your phone can have several folders' worth of pictures.

Figure 5.7
Viewing all the photos from your camera.

So why the difference between these two figures? If you choose Pictures from the Application tab, and you've downloaded a picture from your email or an MMS message, those pictures will be in a separate folder from pictures you've taken with the camera.

Although you can create folders on your SD card with your computer, we can't advise it because it seems to make the camera pretty unreliable. If you do start creating folders on the SD card, we strongly recommend not creating them in the DCIM folder.

If you see several folders of pictures, as in Figure 5.6, tap one of the folders to display all the pictures within that folder, as shown in Figure 5.7. Tap a picture to view it full screen. When you do, two arrows appear on either side of the screen, as shown in Figure 5.8. Just tap them to move from picture to picture. If you wait a second or two, the arrows disappear so that they don't get in the way of your viewing. Just tap the picture again to display them.

Figure 5.8
Viewing your picture full screen.

When you tap the picture, in addition to the arrows, you see zoom buttons at the bottom, as shown in Figure 5.8. Use these buttons to zoom in on a particular area of your picture. Tap and hold one of the buttons to zoom in or out continually.

Viewing a Slideshow of Your Pictures

Your phone can display all your pictures in a slideshow. This can be helpful when you're showing vacation pictures to friends or family. To begin a slideshow, press the Menu button and then tap Slideshow. Each picture is displayed for about 2 seconds, and then the next picture fades in. The slideshow displays each picture once. When all pictures have been displayed, the slideshow ends, and the first picture is displayed.

If you want to pause the slideshow, just tap the screen. The slideshow stops, and the current picture is displayed. To resume the slideshow, press the Menu button and tap Slideshow again.

Basic Picture Options

You can access several other options by pressing the Menu button while viewing a picture:

- **Share:** Just like the sharing functionality described earlier in this chapter, you can send a picture to an email address or phone number.

- **Rotate:** Just tap this option to rotate the picture. Tap Rotate left or Rotate right to rotate the picture.

- **Flip orientation:** Tap this option to change the orientation of the phone's display. The picture won't actually rotate, just the Notification bar at the top of the screen and the location of the Next and Previous buttons and the menu options.

- **Delete:** Tap Delete and then OK to permanently delete the picture.

- **More:** Tap More for some advanced options.

Advanced Picture Options

Pressing the Menu button and tapping More brings up the menu shown in Figure 5.9.

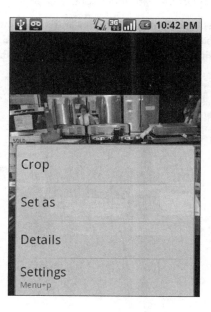

Figure 5.9
Advanced picture options.

Tap Crop to place a crop box around your picture, as shown in Figure 5.10. You can touch the screen and move around the square to select just one area of the photo. Touch one of the yellow lines to display arrows on each line. You can move your finger around the screen to make the yellow box bigger or smaller. When you're done, tap Save, or tap Discard to put the picture back the way it was.

Figure 5.10
Cropping your pictures.

Set as allows you to set your picture as a contact's picture or as your phone's wallpaper, as discussed earlier in the "Taking Pictures with Your Phone" section.

Tapping Details should display information very similar to that shown in Figure 5.11. This information includes the picture's name, file size, resolution, date taken, and, if you've enabled location details, the location where the picture was taken. To hide this box, just press the Back button.

The last option is Settings. We'll cover that in the next section.

Figure 5.11
Picture details.

Customizing Picture Settings

Your phone does lots of cool stuff. Slideshows are great. Your less technically savvy friends or family members will be impressed that your phone can do all that. However, if you're anything like us, you probably want to play around with the picture settings to make your phone even more awesome.

To change your picture settings, press the Menu button, tap More, and then tap Settings to display the screen shown in Figure 5.12.

Picture Size

Your phone's camera is 2 megapixels. This means that each picture you take can be as big as 500KB. Although that's a lot smaller than most new digital cameras, it's still too big to send as an MMS message. Tap Small to reduce the size of your pictures, and then tap OK to save your changes.

If you reduce the size of your pictures, you also reduce their quality. So if you think your pictures are too grainy or fuzzy, switch back to the large picture size.

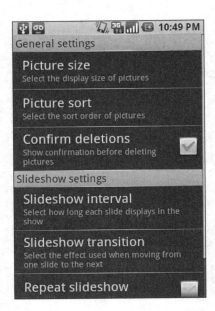

Figure 5.12
You can control a lot of different settings.

Picture Sort

There are only two options here. You can sort your pictures with the newest first or the newest last. Just tap the option you want, and then tap OK.

Confirm Deletions

This is another option that's pretty self-explanatory. If you tap to uncheck this box, tapping Delete on a picture instantly deletes it. There's no warning and no way to undo the deletion, so be careful with this option.

Slideshow Interval

Tap this option to change how long each picture is displayed during the slideshow. The longest interval you can choose is 4 seconds, so you can't use the slideshows to show off your vacation pictures with detailed explanations of the amazing sunsets or interesting plant life. However, increasing the interval will allow people to ooh and aah longer.

Slideshow Transition

Now here's a cool setting. By default, when you are watching a slideshow, one picture fades out, and another fades in. But you can change these effects. Choose from fade, slide, or random. If you choose random, the phone just picks a random effect for each picture. This might get you a few more oohs and aahs.

Repeat Slideshow

Remember how we told you that the slideshow displays each picture only once? Well, just tap the Repeat slideshow option, and the slideshow keeps going until you stop it.

Shuffle Slides

No, this option isn't some new (or old) dance step. Tapping Shuffle slides displays pictures in your slideshow in random order.

Using Your Android-Powered Phone as a Personal Media Player

Listening to Your Music

Personal media players are everywhere these days. Ever since the iPod was released in 2001, more and more people have been carrying around all their music on these little handheld devices. Over the years, our household has probably had at least six different MP3 players between the two of us.

Until recently, if you wanted a personal media player, you needed to carry around a device that was separate from your phone. Over the past few years, though, that's started to change.

Your Android-powered phone comes with a little storage card called a micro secure digital (SD) storage card. This tiny card (it's about one-fourth the size of a postage stamp) can hold up to 8GB worth of data, which is enough to store a lot of songs.

How many songs can you pack into an 8GB SD card? Well, that depends on a lot of things. It depends on the format you use to store your songs, the quality (bit rate) at which they're encoded, how long the songs are, and whether you are using that micro SD card for anything else. As the saying goes, your mileage may vary. The G1 from T-Mobile comes with a 1GB card, but you can find larger cards at a variety of retail stores.

Your Android-powered phone is an excellent music player supporting more formats than you may even know exist, and definitely more than I had ever heard of. We all know about MP3 files, and of course those are supported, but also supported is this fine list of formats:

- **M4A:** This is the iTunes DRM free format.

- **WMA version 8:** This format comes from Microsoft's Windows Media Player.

- **MIDI:** This is what the kids today would call "old School." Best example? Think of Mario Brothers on your Nintendo.

- **WAV:** This is an older sound file format that you run into on Windows-based computers for event sounds, such as new mail, error messages, and the like.

- **OGG Vorbis:** This is an open-source format that is supposed to be of a better quality than MP3. The primary place to find information on it is at www.archive.org/details/audio.

- **AMR:** This particular format is primarily a speech format, as opposed to music. Most commonly, these files come from a voice note-type system.

Playing Music

Your phone comes with a few songs preloaded, so you can begin listening to music right away. The steps are very simple.

Tap the Application tab, and then tap Music to display the screen shown in Figure 6.1.

You can choose from the following options:

- **Artists:** This screen lists all your music grouped by artist. So every song from Flight of the Conchords, for example, is listed together.

- **Albums:** This screen groups all your music by the album that the song is on.

- **Songs:** This is just an alphabetical listing of all the songs on your phone.

- **Playlists:** A playlist is a customized group of songs that you've decided should be played one after another. We'll cover that in just a bit.

Tap any of the options to see a screen that looks something like Figure 6.2.

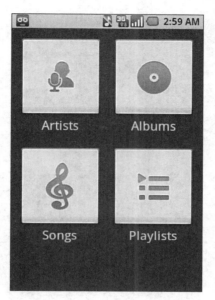

Figure 6.1
Your music is organized in several ways.

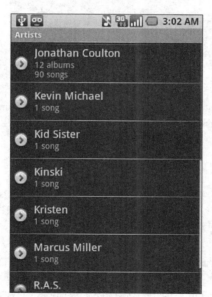

Figure 6.2
Your music grouped by artist.

Just tap one of the entries to start playing the song. Your phone displays a screen something like Figure 6.3.

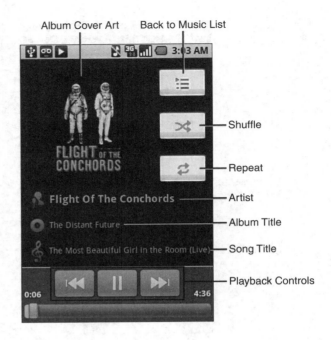

Figure 6.3

Listen to a song and see some information about it.

You can use the volume controls on the left side of the phone to adjust the music volume. This won't change the volume of the ringer, just the music.

Wait! The song's over, but music is still playing! What's up with that? Well, if you chose a song from an album stored on your phone, when that song is done playing, the next song on the album starts playing. Just tap the Pause button if you wanted to hear only that one song.

If, after selecting a specific song, you want to go back to the music list, you can tap the Back to music list button, shown in Figure 6.3, or press the phone's Back button. You see an icon like the one shown in Figure 6.4 next to the song that's playing. Or, if you press the Menu button and tap Music Library, you see at the bottom of the screen what is currently playing.

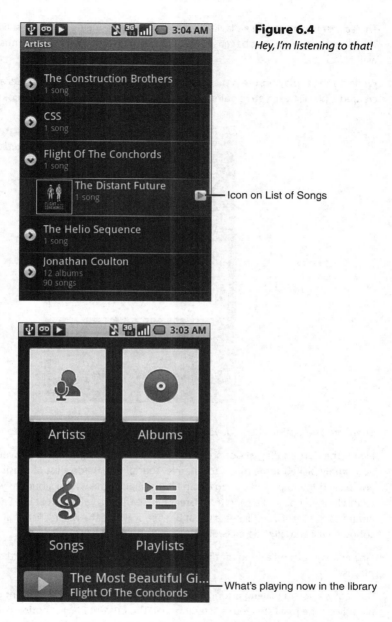

Figure 6.4
Hey, I'm listening to that!

Icon on List of Songs

What's playing now in the library

At this point, you can just navigate through your library and find more songs to play.

Creating and Using Playlists

Playlists are the modern equivalent of the mix tape—that group of songs you just want to
hear together and be able to pull out when you get in that mood.

The easiest way to create a playlist is to start where we are right now, just listening to a song. There are other ways, but because we just walked through how to play music, we might as well start here.

While a song is playing, press the Menu button and tap Add to Playlist. Because you haven't created a playlist yet, you're going to see an Add to Playlist screen that looks like Figure 6.5.

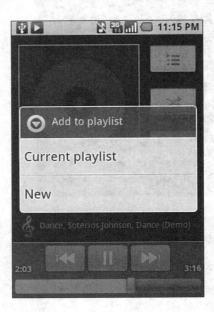

Figure 6.5
Adding to a playlist.

There are two options here for you to choose from, each of which needs a little explaining.

First is the Current Playlist option, which can be a little confusing. You haven't set up a playlist; you simply picked some music to listen to. Your phone made a list of music based on the song you picked. If you picked a song off an album, it adds the whole album to your playlist. For example, if you picked a song from Great Big Sea, it adds all of Great Big Sea's songs from that album to the list. If you picked a Great Big Sea song off the master list of all of Great Big Sea's songs, it willl actually add all Great Big Sea's songs to the list.

Finally, if you picked a song off the master list of all the songs, it adds all the songs to your playlist.

But really, if you're playing a song, you don't want to add it to your current playlist because it's already on the playlist—you're listening to it. The Current Playlist option is far more useful when you've already built a playlist and want to add songs, which we'll talk about in a few pages. For now, select New.

As you can see in Figure 6.6, you can tap the Save button to create a playlist with the very unique name New Playlist 1, or you can actually open up the keyboard and create something a little more intelligently named, as you can see in Figure 6.7.

Figure 6.6
You might want to choose a better name for your playlist.

Figure 6.7
A much better option for naming your playlist.

After you've created the playlist, you probably want to add more songs to your list. To do so, go to your music library and tap and hold on whatever songs you'd like to add, and select Add to Playlist.

As you can see in Figure 6.8, you can create a new playlist from here as well. This is just another way to create a new playlist or add to any playlist you have already created.

Want to see what your list looks like? Go back to the player by pressing the Menu button, tapping Playback, and tapping Current Playlist in the upper right.

Press the Menu button to see what you can do here, as shown in Figure 6.9.

Figure 6.8
Just one more way to create a new playlist.

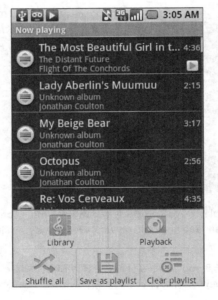

Figure 6.9
You can access your library from the Menu button.

- **Library:** This brings you back to your library.

- **Playback:** This brings you back to the media player.

- **Shuffle all:** Why listen in whatever order is there now? This button mixes up the order of the songs.

- **Save as playlist:** This is the big one. You spend a bunch of time building a playlist; this is where you actually get to save it for future use.

- **Clear playlist:** This clears a current playlist that hasn't been saved. It does not remove items from a saved playlist.

Accessing Saved Playlists

To access your saved playlists, just open the Music application and tap Playlists; you see the screen shown in Figure 6.10. Tap the playlist you want to play, and it immediately starts playing.

Figure 6.10
Pick a playlist, any playlist.

Modifying Saved Playlists

After you've created a playlist, it isn't set in stone. If you get a new album or song and you want to add it to an existing playlist, or you've played that one Gourds song repeatedly and you're tired of it, you can modify a saved playlist to add, remove, or reorganize the songs.

To modify a saved playlist, tap and hold the playlist name and choose Edit. Unfortunately, you can't do much to the playlist other than tapping and holding a song and either deleting it from your phone or removing it from the playlist. You can't reorganize the playlist, because all playlists store the songs in alphabetical order.

Deleting Playlists

It happens. Your tastes change, or you start running rather than cycling, and you need to delete a playlist because it just doesn't work for you anymore. To delete an existing playlist, tap and hold the playlist and select Delete.

Party Shuffle

Although you probably won't use your Android phone to DJ the next party you go to, Party shuffle is a must for anyone who has a large media library. It takes every song in your library and throws them randomly into a list and starts playing.

How great is that?

To access Party shuffle, just press the Menu button from the main music screen or the playback screen, and tap Party shuffle.

Removing Songs from Your Library

It happens. You take an old CD, put all the songs on your computer, and then copy them to your phone. You're grooving to the beats when, all of a sudden, a song comes up and you remember why that CD was collecting dust on your shelf.

Most every group has a stinker or two in their catalog. It happens. Even my favorite groups, like Eddie From Ohio, The Gourds, and Great Big Sea (pause for everyone to say "Who?") have one or two songs that, frankly, I just don't care for. But it's on your phone now! That song you hate. It might remind you of an ex-girlfriend or a bad hangover. It doesn't matter why; you just want to get rid of it.

There's no need to hook the phone back up to your computer. If you are listening to the song right now, press the Menu button and then tap Delete. You're asked if you're sure you want to delete it, as shown in Figure 6.11.

Of course, there's more than one way to delete a song. If you're looking at a song in a list, just tap and hold the song, and tap Delete when the menu comes up. If you're looking at a list of Artists or Albums, you can tap and hold the artist or album and tap Delete when it comes up. You have to delete songs one at a time.

Purchasing New Songs

Although you can always take songs off CDs and put them on your computer, and then your phone, you also can buy music in electronic format. You can do that from your computer, but that's not what we're all about. We're all about your phone. Sure enough, you can do that here too.

Figure 6.11
When deleting a song, you need to confirm that you really want it gone.

First, return to the home screen. If you want to keep listening to music, you can do that too. Open the Applications tab and tap Amazon MP3 to display the screen shown in Figure 6.12.

Figure 6.12
Welcome to Amazon!

The options are pretty straightforward. Top 100 Albums and Top 100 Songs are based on purchase frequency and popularity. You can choose Browse by Genre when you're in the mood to buy some random Live Folk.

Overall, the process is straightforward until you tap the price to buy a song. The price changes to a Buy button. Tap that, and you get the error message shown in Figure 6.13.

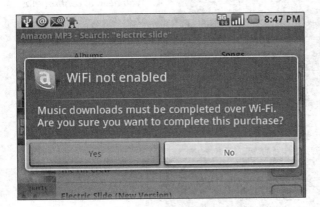

Figure 6.13
Oops! You must be connected to Wi-Fi.

You can't actually buy music over the cell phone network. This requires a Wi-Fi network, like you would find in a coffee shop, or maybe at home. So, tap Yes to tell the phone you want to buy the song. The next time you connect to Wi-Fi, the song will download. If you don't want to buy the song, tap No.

To say that you have to connect to Wi-Fi to purchase a song isn't completely accurate. You actually can purchase the song with no issues. What you can't do is download the song. Note that you also need an Amazon account to purchase music.

We haven't talked about how to connect to a Wi-Fi network; we're saving that for a little later. So if you want, skip ahead to Chapter 10, "Using Wi-Fi," and learn how to configure Wi-Fi on your phone. Otherwise, read on!

After you're connected to Wi-Fi, if you've already purchased music but haven't downloaded it, launch Amazon MP3 again, and press the Menu button and tap Downloads. The tracks should automatically download for you.

Using Songs as Ringtones

You're listening to music, and a song comes up, and you think to yourself, "That song reminds me of my best friend. I wish my phone could sound like that every time she calls me."

Your thought is our command. Well, okay, it's the phone's command; we're just here to tell you about it.

First you need to select the song as your default ringtone. Don't worry if you don't want the song to play for every incoming call from every contact. This is just a temporary measure to add the song to the list of available ringtones. Tap and hold the song's name, and choose Use as phone ringtone. You see a message letting you know that the phone's ringtone has changed. Follow these steps to complete the process:

1. Head back to Settings (on the Application tab) and tap **Sound & display** to display the screen shown in Figure 6.14.

Figure 6.14

Edit your sound settings to pick a ringtone.

2. Tap **Phone ringtone**, and choose a ringtone to use as the default.

3. You're almost back where you started. Press the **Home** button to exit the Settings application.

The last part of the process is to actually associate your chosen song with a particular contact. To do this, follow these steps:

1. Open your contacts, and scroll to the contact you want.

2. Tap and hold the contact's name, and then choose **Edit contact** from the pop-up menu.

3. Scroll down to the **Other information** section, as shown in Figure 6.15.

4. Tap the **Ringtone** drop-down to select a custom ringtone for the contact. Tap **OK** when you're done.

5. Press the **Menu** button, and tap **Save** to save your changes.

Figure 6.15
Every contact can have his or her own ringtone.

The authors deny any responsibility for bodily injury should you set your wife's ringtone to "Baby Got Back."

Copying Songs to Your Phone

If you've bought music online before, or if you own a bunch of CDs and you want to transfer them to your phone, the easiest way to do this is by copying the music from your computer to your phone. Follow these steps to connect your phone to your computer and copy music files to the phone:

1. Plug your phone into the computer using the USB cable that came with the phone.

2. Tap and pull down the **status bar**, and then tap the **USB connected - Select to copy files to/from your computer** option, as shown in Figure 6.16.

3. If you're using Windows Vista, open the Computer folder; you'll see your phone listed as a drive. This means it's available for you to move files to. If you're using a Mac, an icon for the phone should appear on your desktop somewhere. Double-click the phone's icon to open a window just for the phone.

4. Find the folder on your computer that has your music, and open it.

5. Drag any music files you want to move from the **Music** folder on your computer to the music folder on the phone.

When you're done, just unplug the phone, and you're ready to rock.

Figure 6.16

USB connected to computer and phone.

Watching Videos

First, we should discuss the bad news.

At the time this book went to press, Android-powered phones didn't support playing a video that you have stored on your SD card out of the box. It's possible that in the future, a video player might come preinstalled on your phone.

But there is good news as well.

The good news is that, as discussed in Chapter 9, "Adding New Applications," other people can (and have) written their own video players that you can download and install. These applications are available from the Android Market. Unfortunately, because these applications are not supplied by Google or the phone manufacturers, there is no guarantee that the applications that are available today will be available tomorrow.

➔   For more information on finding and installing applications on your phone, **see** "Finding and Installing New Applications," **p. 150**.

The Joy of YouTube

Maybe you haven't heard of YouTube. In case you're not one of the 130 million unique monthly users, YouTube is an Internet website where normal, everyday people can upload videos to share with other users. Between the customer-created videos, you'll find "official" videos from the likes of the BBC, Barack Obama, and the NBA. That description just about sums it up—for the sanitized version, at least.

The less sanitized version is that YouTube is, by and large, a black hole that will suck in your time as you watch video after video. One video will make you laugh, one video will make you wonder how to get your time back, and sometimes that is the same video. YouTube is fun and amusing, but sometimes it is just plain boring.

Your phone comes with easy access to YouTube, now owned by Google. As long as you have a strong signal, watching videos on your mobile phone is easy, quick, and highly entertaining.

Playing a YouTube Video

We'll start by launching the YouTube application and finding a few videos to watch. Follow these steps:

1. Tap the **Application** tab, scroll down, and tap **YouTube**.

2. Tap **Most Popular** to display a screen something like what you see in Figure 6.17.

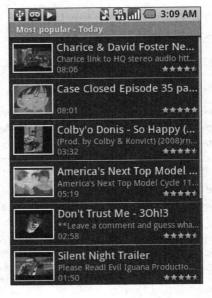

Figure 6.17
You can choose from YouTube's most popular videos.

3. Tap a video to play it.

Because this list is continually in flux, your list of the most popular videos probably won't look like ours.

If you want to pause the video while you're watching it, just tap the phone's screen to bring up the controls shown in Figure 6.18.

Figure 6.18
You have some control over the video playback.

If you receive a phone call while listening to music or watching a YouTube video, your phone interrupts the video to allow you to answer the call.

Tap the pause button to pause the video, the play button to restart the video, or the rewind and fast-forward buttons to move through the video. You'll also notice a status bar that shows you exactly how long the video is, how much of it you've watched, and how much time is left.

Some videos are so funny, strange, or amazing that you want to watch a few seconds of them repeatedly. You can do this by tapping the screen to display the DVD player-like controls, tapping and holding the progress bar, and sliding the whole bar back a bit. Tap the play button, and your video starts again from the point you just selected.

To return to the YouTube application, you can do one of three things:

- Wait for your current video to finish playing.
- Press the Back button on the phone.
- Press the Menu button, and then tap Home Page.

When your video finishes playing, you see a screen much like the one shown in Figure 6.19.

Here you can choose to watch another video that might be related to the video you just watched. For example, if you're a fan of the "Will It Blend?" series, where a wide variety of everyday items are thrown in an industrial blender, you can use the trackball to scroll through the various "Will It Blend?" videos and choose another one to watch. However, if you want to do something else, press the Menu button, and then tap Home Page.

Figure 6.19
Did you like that video? Pick another.

YouTube Categories

If you can't figure out what to watch, or you're in the mood for a particular type of video, just press the Menu button and tap Categories to display the screen shown in Figure 6.20.

Figure 6.20
Choose from a variety of categories.

Scroll through the list and tap any category that interests you to see a list of videos from that category.

Searching for YouTube Videos

You've heard of the "Will It Blend?" videos, and you want to see more. But only a couple of them are on the popular videos list. Well, you can search for videos by name very easily.

1. Press the **Menu** button and tap **Search**. You see something similar to Figure 6.21.

Figure 6.21
Like most Android search screens, this one shows a list of your recent searches.

2. Type your search term, and then tap **Search** to display the results, as shown in Figure 6.22.

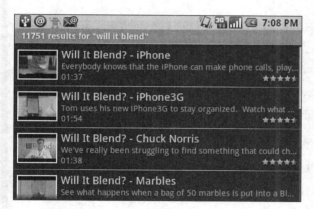

Figure 6.22
Tap the video you want to watch.

3. Scroll through the list of results, and tap the video you want to watch.

Accessing Video Details

Saying that YouTube has a lot of different videos is like saying that Seattle is a little wet in the winter (or in the summer, for that matter). As soon as you've started watching a video, you might wonder about its creator, or even what the video is about. Luckily there is a handy way to do that. While the video is either playing or paused, press the Menu button and tap Details to display something similar to Figure 6.23.

Figure 6.23
So who made that video, anyway?

On the Details screen, you can view all the information that the video owner saw fit to enter. Some video owners enter a detailed summary, and others enter just the most basic information, such as the title.

As you scroll through the details, you see a summary of the video that includes the following information:

- **Star rating and view data:** Every time you watch a video on YouTube, you can give it a rating of one to six stars.

- **Length:** This is the video's total playing time.

- **Publisher:** This is the YouTube user who created and uploaded the video.

- **Added:** This is the date that the video was uploaded to YouTube.

- **URL:** This is the URL that takes you directly to the video in a web browser.

Scroll down even farther for a list of related videos.

If you scroll through the related videos, you'll notice that your phone pauses. YouTube has so many videos that almost any video you choose will have a very long list of related videos. To minimize the amount of data your phone downloads, the YouTube application loads only a few of these at a time. Just keep scrolling down, and your phone will download a few more every time you scroll.

Commenting on Videos

Ah, commenting. We are nothing if not a world of critics, and YouTube allows anyone who watches a video to leave a comment. Do you like a video? Leave a comment! Do you hate a video? You can leave a comment then too. We've uploaded a few cooking videos to YouTube, and although some of the comments are just spam, some of the response we've gotten have been very interesting.

While the video is either paused or playing, press the Menu button, and then tap Comments. Be aware that, as in life, some people who comment on YouTube videos don't leave the most polite comments, so view these at your own risk.

Choosing Your Favorite Videos

You're actually rolling on the floor laughing. Tears are streaming down your face. You've just watched the funniest video you've ever seen. You want to watch this video every day for a year. You want to watch it every time you're sad or upset. You love this video.

If you really love a video and want to make it easily accessible, just add it to your favorites. Press the Menu button and tap Favorites. That's it! You see a quick message telling you that the video has been added to your favorites.

Now that you have a few favorites, how do you access them? After all, saving a video doesn't do you much good if you can't get back to it. From the YouTube application's home screen, press the Menu button and tap Favorites. You see something like Figure 6.24. Just tap a video to play it.

Figure 6.24
Easily access your favorite videos.

Sharing Videos

Remember that amazingly funny video? You want to share it with all your friends. You probably want to shout the video from the rooftops, but those URLs are pretty long and probably should be emailed rather than shouted.

To share a video, press the Menu button and tap Share. Your phone displays a new email message with the subject and message body already filled in. Just type in an address (or two or three) and tap Send. You can also change the subject or message body if you want.

Accessing YouTube Settings

There's one last option you can access by pressing the Menu button from the YouTube home page—Settings. This option doesn't do much, though. Tap Clear Search history to, well, clear your search history. When you're done with that, you need to press the Back button on your phone to return to the home page.

Using the Internet

The Internet. The World Wide Web. More than just a series of tubes, the Internet is a wild and wonderful entity that we hope will never become self-aware. You can find just about anything on the Internet.

Do you want dried loganberries? The Internet can tell you where to buy them.

Do you want to know when the iPod was invented? Easy. Just type "when was the iPod invented" into a search box, and within a couple of clicks, you'll have the full scoop.

Do you need the phone number of that new coffee shop down the street? Just look it up.

Just like on your PC, you can access almost anything on the Internet with your Android-powered phone.

Accessing the Browser

You have several different ways to access the Internet. You can open the browser and type a word or phrase into the Google Search box, or you can click a link in an email message.

To access the browser, just tap Browser on the home screen. You can also tap the Application tab and then tap Browser. Either way brings up the browser, as shown in Figure 7.1.

Figure 7.1
The browser allows you to access the Internet.

As you're reading through this chapter, you might notice that some of your favorite websites just don't load the same way on your phone as they do on your computer. Some scripts don't load on the phone, and some animation won't display properly either. If your favorite website doesn't load well on your phone, contact the site's webmaster, and tell him or her that a mobile-friendly page would be greatly appreciated.

Opening a Website by Typing a URL

Flip open your phone and press the Menu button; you see a Go to URL option. Tap that, and you end up with a screen that looks a little something like Figure 7.2.

Figure 7.2
To all the sites I've seen before.

You see a list of websites you've visited before. If you're planning to go to a site you visit regularly, you'll probably see it listed here. If it is listed, just tap it, and the site loads.

If the site you want to go to isn't listed, just start typing the address you want. Your phone remembers the websites you have visited in the past, and will suggest websites that match the characters you've entered in the URL box. If you've been to the site before, you'll see it on the list, as seen in the upper section of Figure 7.3. If you've never been there before, your phone gives you the option of using Google to search for something, as shown in the lower section of Figure 7.3.

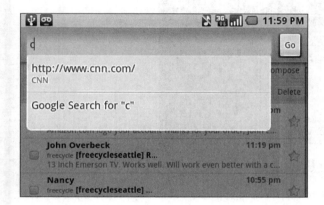

Figure 7.3
Entering the website you want to go to or a term to search for.

After you finish typing the URL, you can press the Enter key on the keyboard or tap the Go button on the screen.

Viewing More Than One Website at a Time

Sometimes you need to have two different websites open. Perhaps you're reading an article, and you come across a word whose definition you don't know. Or perhaps you want to check the score of the big game. Simply press the Menu button and tap Window.

Tap New window, and just browse as you normally do. When you need to go back to the other browser window, press the Menu button and tap Window, and then tap the window you want. If you need another new window, tap New window again.

Your screen probably will start to look something like Figure 7.4.

If you get to the point that you are so far down the screen that you can't see the New window icon, you can press the Menu button and tap New window.

If you want to close a window, you can tap the X button in the Windows view. Or, when looking at a web page, press the Menu button, tap More, and then tap Close.

Figure 7.4
With this many windows, there better be a nice view.

Checking a Page for Content Updates

Not every website is fancy enough to update changing information as you read. If you're viewing baseball scores, your phone might not refresh the page automatically every time one
team scores a run. Add in the fact that some sites can't do their fancy things on your mobile
phone's browser, and sometimes you need to force your phone to refresh a page. Fortunately
that's an easy task. When you're looking at the page, press the Menu button and tap Refresh.

Moving Through History

We've all been there. You're on a news site, and you tap a link to read an article. Then you do it
again to view another article. Then you decide to go back to the first site to read another
article.

So how do you get back without retyping the URL? Press the Menu button, tap More, and tap
Back. You also can press the Menu button and J at the same time to do the same thing. And if
you need to go forward again, it's the same route. Just tap Forward, or press the Menu button
and K together.

There's No Place Like Home

When you fire up the web browser, you see Google's home page. Although that's all well and
good, as you'll see in a bit, you have quite a few ways to search, so maybe you want to set your
default page to be something other than Google search. Follow these steps to change your
home page:

1. Press the **Menu** button.

2. Tap **More**.

3. Scroll through the list to **Settings**.

4. Tap **Set home page** to display the screen shown in Figure 7.5.

Figure 7.5
You can choose any web page for your home page.

5. Type in the URL you want to use.

Now, whenever you want to go back to your home page, you can press the Menu button, tap More, and then tap Home page.

Sharing Web Pages with Others

Sometimes you land on a page that you really want to share with someone. To do so, follow these steps:

1. Press the **Menu** button.

2. Tap **More**.

3. Tap **Share Page**.

These steps start a new email message in Gmail with the URL already in the message body. At this point, it's just an email message, and you already know how to send a message.

➔   For more information about sending and receiving email, **see** "Sending a New Message," **p. 68**.

Zooming to a Better View

Some web pages are a little hard to read on your phone, so you'll be happy to know that your phone's web browser has some zoom functionality. It's pretty tricky to describe without holding the phone in front of you and showing you in person, but we'll do our best.

First, let's load a website. Because I'm very familiar with its content, we'll load the website www.cooklocal.com. You know how to get there. As soon as it's up, you'll see that it doesn't fit the screen very well. You can touch the screen and drag your finger around to move around the web page. When you do that, you see three buttons fade into view at the bottom, as shown in Figure 7.6.

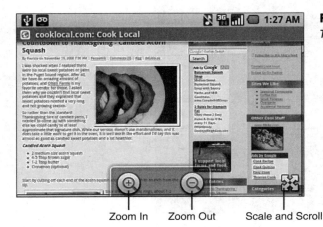

Zoom In   Zoom Out   Scale and Scroll

Figure 7.6

The zoom buttons.

The Zoom in and Zoom out buttons are pretty self-evident, so we'll focus on the Scale and Scroll button. Give it a tap. You see something like the screen shown in Figure 7.7.

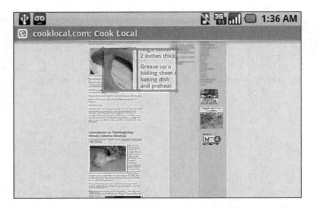

Figure 7.7

Use the Scale and Scroll button to select part of a hard-to-read web page that you want to zoom in on.

Tap and hold near the zoomed-in box, and drag your finger around the shrunken screen. You should see a zoomed-in image of what is beneath the box. When you're zoomed in where you want to read the page, let go of the screen, and you're zoomed in to that spot.

Creating and Using Bookmarks

No doubt you have quite a few favorite websites you visit regularly. Maybe you're like me, and you load quite a few websites on your phone. That's what Bookmarks are for. Just like you use a bookmark in a book to find the page where you left off, a bookmark in your web browser lets you find a site that you want to be able to get back to easily. Bookmarks are stored in a list that the phone calls Favorites.

After you've opened a web page, press the Menu button, tap Bookmarks, and then tap New Bookmark.

If you want to open one of your favorites, press the Menu button, tap Bookmarks, and tap the bookmark you want to open.

To delete a bookmark you no longer need, press the Menu button and tap Bookmarks. Tap and hold the bookmark you'd like to delete, and select Delete bookmark.

You might have noticed other options when you looked at how to delete a bookmark:

- **Open:** This opens the bookmark, or loads it in the browser.

- **Open in a new window:** This opens the bookmark in a new browser window.

- **Edit bookmark:** You can change the bookmark's name or location (also known as the URL).

- **Share link:** This composes a new email with the bookmark's URL in the body.

- **Copy link URL:** This allows you to paste the URL somewhere, such as an email message body or a text message. After you've copied the link URL, simply tap and hold where you want the URL to go, and select Paste.

Google Search

This is what Google is known for: searching the Web. With Google Search, your phone is the key to the world in your pocket—figuratively speaking, at least.

Searching for Websites

There are a few different ways to search Google. You can do so from the home screen: just scroll to the right, enter your search term, and press Enter. You can open the web browser, press the Menu button, and tap Search. Or you can just go to Google.com in your web browser.

Type what you want to search for in the box, and press Enter.

When you start typing, you see a drop-down list of some common terms matching the letters you've entered so far, as shown in Figure 7.8.

Figure 7.8
The Google screen.

This process is like autocomplete, but it uses logic inside Google to figure out what you might be searching for. If what you want appears in the list, tap it. Otherwise, keep typing until you've finished what you want to search for, and then press Enter.

Searching for Images

When you load Google.com, you see four options just above the search box, as shown in Figure 7.9.

Figure 7.9
Where else can I go from here?

If you tap Images, you can search for—you guessed it—images. Let's try searching for lilacs.

The results we found as we wrote this chapter likely will be different from what you see, but your results might look something like Figure 7.10.

Figure 7.10
Lilacs, the very image of spring.

If you see an image you like, tap and hold the picture, and then tap Save image. The image is saved to your phone's memory. You can access it by launching the Pictures application.

Local Searches

The Local search sandwiched between Photos and News is like a local phone book. You can search for restaurants, appliance stores—whatever you'd normally pick up a phone book to look for. Google gives you addresses, phone numbers, and, on occasion, customer ratings.

Searching for News

At the far right of Figure 7.9, you see the News search option. This lets you search for news items on a certain topic. Try tapping the News link and searching for the name of your favorite sports team, favorite movie star, or favorite writer.

Google pulls from newspapers, news wires—any source possible to provide you with up-to-date information about whatever you search for.

Advanced Web Browser Settings

Even though the web browser is very functional as it is, you might want to tweak a few settings or view a few of the more advanced features it supports.

Managing Your History

Your browser keeps a history of where you've been. This feature comes in handy when you can't find a page you viewed a while ago. Load the Internet browser, press the Menu button, tap More, and then tap History. You see something like Figure 7.11.

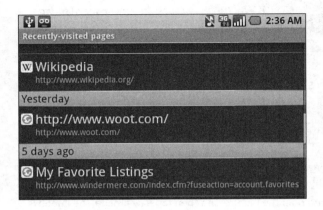

Figure 7.11
The past is always 20/20.

This list is much the same as your bookmarks list. Tapping and holding gives you the same options—Open, Open in a new window, and so on. The only difference is the Remove from history command.

Suppose you want to get rid of your browsing history. Maybe you borrowed your loved one's phone to do some online holiday shopping. Maybe you accidentally typed in a domain name that is very close to one of your favorites but wasn't what you intended. If you want to clear your entire history, follow these steps:

1. From within the browser, press the **Menu** button, tap **More**, scroll down, and tap **Settings**.

2. Scroll down to the **Privacy settings** options, as shown in Figure 7.12, and tap **Clear history**.

3. Tap **OK** to the warning message that all the browser navigation history will be cleared.

Finding Your Downloads

Sometimes a website has something you want. Maybe it's an image you really like, maybe it's a program you need to install, or maybe it's a file that someone has posted on a website. Whatever the reason, if you've downloaded anything from a website while on your mobile phone, the phone has a record of it.

Although such record-keeping may sound uncomfortably like Big Brother, it's not meant to be. The download history allows you to easily access any files you've downloaded without having to search for them. Just press the Menu button and then tap More. Tap Downloads to display the screen shown in Figure 7.13.

Figure 7.12
You really can forget the past.

Figure 7.13
How much have you downloaded?

To access a file you downloaded, just tap it, and the file opens. To remove it from the list, tap and hold the file's icon, and choose Clear from list. This doesn't actually delete the file; it just removes it from the Download history.

Browser Settings

But wait! There's more! As with the web browser on your computer, you can control a wide variety of settings on your phone's web browser, as shown in Figure 7.14.

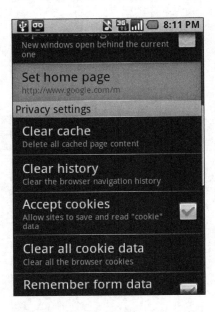

Figure 7.14
Use these options to configure your web browser.

The following sections detail the various settings you can configure to adjust your web browsing experience to your liking.

Page Content Settings

These settings affect how pages look and act when you are viewing websites:

- **Text size:** Tap this option to change the display size of text on the page.
- **Block pop-up windows:** Some websites like to open new windows when you load them. Many do this to display advertisements, but some use this for functionality. If you don't like multiple windows opening when you didn't request them, tap to check this box.
- **Load images:** If you don't have an unlimited data plan, or you're in the desert and you don't have a very good connection, you can tap to disable images. This can help your web pages load faster, but it might also break some functionality and make the web pages look a bit odd.
- **Auto-fit pages:** Your phone's screen, although big for a phone, is a lot smaller than the one on your computer. Tap this option to make sure that all web pages resize themselves to fit on your phone's screen.

- **Enable JavaScript:** This option sounds technical and advanced. Well, it is technical. JavaScript is a programming language that allows web pages to do some cool stuff. It's generally okay, so you can leave this option checked.

- **Open in background:** Sometimes, when you tap a link on a web page, it opens in a new window. Sometimes, if you tap and hold a link, you can select Open in a new window. When either of these things happens, this setting means that the new window isn't actually visible. It's "behind" the window you're looking at. Just go through to Windows to find it.

- **Set home page:** Earlier we discussed how to set your home page, so we'll skip that for now.

Privacy Settings

Privacy is an important concern because of the threat of identity theft. The settings here don't really protect you too much, but they are there, and they are better than nothing. Let's see what we have.

- **Clear cache:** Your phone caches the web pages you read. It helps the pages you read load faster when you go back to them. Not all pages support this feature, because things such as news sites depend on the content's being fresh and up to date. But tapping Clear cache gets rid of everything. So no one can see that site you were browsing last night.

- **Clear history:** Clearing the cache isn't enough. You saw earlier that every site you've been to is listed on your phone. Going back to that site you visited last night? Tap Clear history so that no one will see it sitting in your history cache.

- **Accept cookies:** Cookies are a way for a website to store information about you. This could be the contents of an online shopping cart, or which city you're in. Either way, some people see this as a security risk, because any other site could pull that information from your browser. Check this option to accept cookies; uncheck it to not accept them.

- **Clear all cookie data:** If you want to get rid of all the cookies on your phone, just tap this option. Be warned that none of the stored cookie information will remain on your phone, so you might need to reenter some of that information.

- **Remember form data:** On the one hand, this is an exceedingly useful feature. You don't have to type in your mailing address every time you load a form that is be set up properly. At the same time, this would be a way for someone to pull your information and possibly steal your identity. For what it's worth, I leave this option checked.

- **Clear form data:** You can remove all the form data that's saved using the preceding option by tapping this option.

Security Settings

The difference between security and privacy is a thin gray line. Loose privacy leads to a very insecure system. That's why you shred your private papers. No security leads to a lack of privacy. That's why we have blinds and curtains on our windows.

- **Remember passwords:** This is a handy feature for websites that don't keep you logged in using cookies. But anyone who picks up your phone could just log into whatever websites you log into.
- **Clear passwords:** This removes all the usernames and passwords saved on your phone.
- **Show security warnings:** This option lets you know if there's a problem with a site's security, such as a problem with the security certificate, or something a little off with the URLs on the page.

Advanced Settings

This is where we get into the deep stuff.

- **Enable Gears:** Gears is a bit of software that Google created to live in your browser and help websites do much more powerful things, such as allowing you to read blogs when you have no Internet connection. Because Gears is part of Google, Google has made sure that the web browser on your phone can use it too, so long as you check this box.
- **Gears settings:** If you haven't installed any applications that use Gears, you see a box that looks something like Figure 7.15.

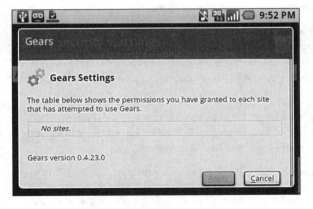

Figure 7.15
There's not much you can do here if you don't have Gears installed.

But let's install a sample application so that you can see how Gears works. In your browser, go to http://code.google.com/apis/gears/sample.html. Tap the Shortcut Demo link, and then tap Create Desktop Shortcut. You see the pop-up shown in Figure 7.16.

Figure 7.16
Giving Gears permission.

When you tap Yes, you see a monkey face icon on your desktop. Tapping it takes you to the Shortcut Demo web page. We'll talk about how to get the monkey off your desktop in Chapter 9, "Adding New Applications," when we talk about adding applications to your phone.

- **Reset to default:** This option undoes all the settings you've set—all the cookies, all the form data, everything. Your phone goes back to the way it was when you first got it. And yes, you are asked if you're sure. This will be a rare occurrence (we hope), but sometimes it's the only way to fix a problem with your phone.

That's about it for configuration settings. In the next chapter you'll learn more about using the Google Application suite.

Using the Rest of the Google Application Suite

Google is much more than just Search. We've already talked about YouTube, Photo Search, News Search, Calendar, Gmail, and Contacts. I'll point you to www.google.com/m/products for other applications that aren't on your phone by default but are configured to be specially formatted for your mobile phone, in your browser. But first I'd like to talk about a couple other applications that do come with your phone.

Google Talk

This phone is all about communication, which seems funny to say about a phone. Of course it's all about communication. You can call and email friends and send them text or picture messages.

You can also send them an instant message (IM). Instant messaging is great for quick interaction with your contacts.

Enough chitchat; let's play.

First, tap the Application tab, and then tap IM. You get a screen like the one shown in Figure 8.1.

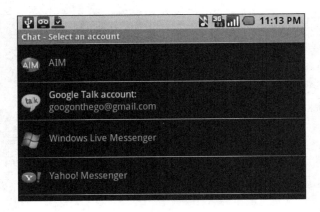

Figure 8.1
Google Talk and other IM applications.

You probably notice that more than Google Talk is listed here. AIM (AOL Instant Messenger), Windows Live Messenger, and Yahoo! Messenger all are available from your phone. Right now, we'll discuss setting up Google Talk, but after that, we'll look at the others.

Tap Google Talk and you see a list of your friends, as shown in Figure 8.2.

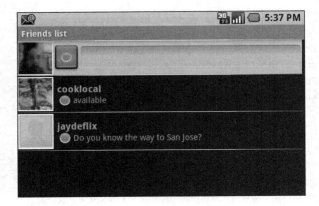

Figure 8.2
Your friends.

Users with a green dot next to their name are online, ones with an orange dot are away, a red dot means busy, and gray means offline.

Here are some things you can do right away:

- To change your status, tap the green dot next to your name.
- To change your picture, tap the gray picture next to the dot, and pick a new picture.
- To add text, such as a witty saying or what you ate for lunch, so that people see something next to your name, you can type it in the gray area next to the dot.

After doing all that, you end up with something that looks like Figure 8.3.

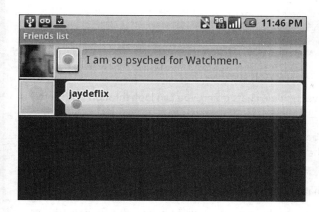

Figure 8.3
Now that's a personalized chat window!

Adding Friends

Yes, I have only one friend—me. You might not have any yet. If you don't, feel free to add me, googonthego@gmail.com.

But I bet you want to know how to do that, right? Just follow these steps:

1. Press the **Menu** button.

2. Tap **Add friend**.

3. Type in the address of the person you'd like to invite to chat.

Chatting with a Friend

Starting a chat is easy. Tap the friend you'd like to chat with, or tap and hold and select Start chat. You end up with a chat window. You type what you want to say at the bottom and read what gets said in the upper window, as shown in Figure 8.4.

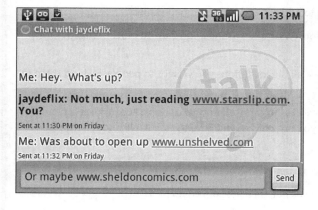

Figure 8.4
Chatting about webcomics. On a Friday night.

More IM Fun

Press the Menu button to find out what else you can do:

- **Friends list:** This brings you back to your chat list.

- **Switch chats:** When you have multiple chats going, you can look through this list to choose one.

- **Add to chat:** A nice thing about Google Talk is that it's a party line. You can add anyone else on your friends list to the chat so that you can all discuss where to get dinner before catching a movie tonight.

- **Close chat:** This ends the chat. Surprised?

- **Insert smiley:** Smileys are a way to show emotions using colons, dashes, parentheses, and other characters. As soon as you get to know them well enough, you'll remember that you can put in a smile with : -) or a frown with : - (, and you won't need to use this option anymore. When you're adding smilies on the phone, they'll actually be the little Android alien smiling or frowning. Note that if the person you're chatting with isn't using Android, she won't see the little green alien. She might see just the : -), or her client might show her something different.

For now, go back to the Friends list, either by closing this chat or by putting it in the background by tapping Friends list.

Friends List Options

Press the Menu button and take a look at the options you have here:

- **Most popular:** This filters your list to the people you talk to the most.

- **Switch chats:** Just like in the chat, this option lets you pick from all your open chats to find one you want.

- **Add friend:** This allows you to add a friend, as mentioned earlier.

- **Blocked:** This shows only blocked contacts. Don't know how to block someone? Keep reading.

- **Invites:** This allows you to see all the invitations you've sent to people, inviting them to be your friend.

- **More:** This option gives you access to three additional options. Account list is pictured in Figure 8.1. Sign out signs you out of Chat and Settings. We'll talk about Settings in a bit.

You also can tap and hold a contact to get even more options:

- **Start chat:** If you're already in a chat, this says Join chat.

- **Friend info:** This shows you your friend's profile.

- **Go to (website):** If the contact has a website listed on her profile, you can open the website right here.

- **Block friend:** Someone bugging you, but he's still your friend, so you don't want him permanently gone? Just tap Block friend. You can unblock him by pulling up your blocked friends.

- **Remove friend:** This pulls the person off your list—until you add him again.

- **Add to Contacts:** Just because you've set up your friend in Google Talk, it doesn't mean he's actually in your contacts.

- **Pin/Unpin friend:** This adds him to/removes him from your Most Popular list.

- **Hide friend:** When you hide a friend, it's not quite as fun as putting him in a car trunk or under a blanket. It simply means that he will never show up on the Most Popular list.

Instant Messaging Settings

We mentioned Settings earlier, so let's cover them now. To access the IM Settings, press the Menu button with the IM application on-screen, and then tap Settings to display the screen shown in Figure 8.5.

Figure 8.5
Change settings for your instant messaging application.

The settings you can configure are as follows:

- **Automatically sign in:** This option, which is checked by default, signs you into the Instant Messaging application whenever you open it. If you want to be able to open the application without signing in, tap to uncheck this option.

- **Mobile indicator:** This option, also checked by default, puts a little indicator next to your name in your friends' chat lists. Keeping this option enabled lets your friends know that you're chatting on a mobile phone and, therefore, your typing might be a little slow and error-prone.

- **IM notifications:** This option places a notification icon in the status bar whenever you get an instant message, as shown in Figure 8.6.

Instant Message Icon

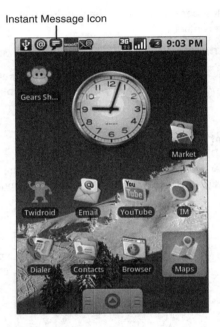

Figure 8.6

The IM notification icon lets you know you have a message waiting.

- **Select ringtone:** This option allows you to pick a ringtone to use whenever you receive an instant message. Tap this option to choose a ringtone.

- **Vibrate:** This option causes the phone to vibrate whenever you receive an instant message.

Other Instant Message Programs

You probably noticed that Figure 8.1 showed more than just Google Talk. Although the main topic of this chapter is Google applications, why don't we take a moment to talk about the other IM options?

AIM, Windows Live Messenger, and Yahoo! Messenger are three other popular instant messaging systems. Maybe you already have accounts on them, or maybe you don't, but setting them up is always roughly the same. So rather than telling you about each one individually, we'll show you how to set one up.

Adding an Account

We'll go through setting up an AIM account. Open the IM application if you aren't already in it. If you are in it, you need to get to the Account list.

If you're looking at a chat, press the Menu button and tap Friends list.

If you're already looking at the Friends list, press the Menu button and tap Account list.

Because we'll set up AIM (AOL's instant messaging application), tap that. As you can see, we're already set up on the other available instant messaging application.

When setting up a new connection, you're presented with a pretty basic logon box, as shown in Figure 8.7.

Figure 8.7
Setting up an AIM account.

If you don't already have an account on whatever system you want to connect to, the logon screen includes a link to create an account. In the case of AIM, as you can see, it is Get a Screen Name. The link is in the same location regardless of the account, but it might say something a little different for each service.

If you don't have an account and you need to create one, tap the link. Doing so opens the appropriate page in a web browser to allow you to create the account.

If you do have an account, just fill in the account name and password.

If you want your phone to remember your password, check the box. If you do, you get a friendly reminder to change your password using your computer should your phone get stolen or lost, as shown in Figure 8.8.

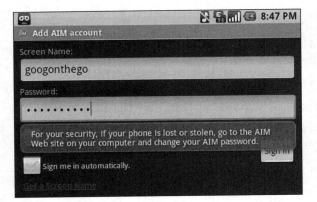

Figure 8.8
*A friendly reminder that storing
your password on your phone does
carry some risks.*

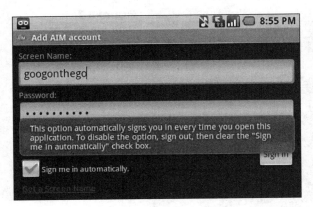

Choose Sign me in automatically if you want the application to sign you in automatically
whenever you launch it. This also comes with a friendly warning, also shown in Figure 8.8.

When you're ready to sign in, simply tap the Sign in button.

Frequent Chatting

After you've used the instant messenger application a bit, you'll find that the Account screen
handily tells you how many chats you have going on in which instant messaging account, as
shown in Figure 8.9. This is a helpful reminder if you are engaged in multiple conversations at
once.

Also helpful is the icon on the Notification bar showing you that an instant message is waiting
for you. When you pull down the Notification list, you see the waiting messages. Or, if you're
particularly popular, you see a list of how many unread messages you have, as shown in Figure
8.10.

Figure 8.9
Someone is a little chatty.

Figure 8.10
People like me—they really like me!

Removing an Account

Let's say you added a Yahoo! account and then realized that you wanted to add a completely different Yahoo! account. Or maybe you were just experimenting with creating an account, and now you want to use a different account.

Head back to the Accounts screen, tap and hold the account you'd like to remove, and select Remove account from the list. That's all there is to it.

Google Maps

A wise man once said "No matter where you go, there you are."

With Google maps and the GPS on this phone, no matter where "there" is, you'll know where you are.

Let's start with the basics. Maps may be on your main screen already, so you can tap it from there. If it isn't, tap the Applications tab, and tap Maps from there.

Do you want the phone to show you where you are? Press the Menu button and tap My Location. If you haven't configured the Location settings to allow the phone to figure out where it is, you get a notification message much like the one shown in Figure 8.11.

Figure 8.11
You can't tell where you are without first configuring the Location settings.

You could tap Cancel here, but that wouldn't tell you where you are. So instead, tap OK; you see two options for your location sources.

First, you could use wireless networks. This option tries to use your mobile phone network to determine your position. Or, if you've already configured Wi-Fi connectivity, despite our not discussing it yet, and you're connected to your Wi-Fi network, your phone uses that to determine your physical location.

→   For more information on Wi-Fi connectivity, **see** Chapter 10, "Using Wi-Fi."

However, if you've enabled the GPS functionality, and you have a good signal to the GPS satellites, your phone zooms right in on where you are currently located.

On the other hand, if you don't have a good signal, or the Wi-Fi or mobile networks aren't helping you figure out where you are, you end up with an error message like the one shown in Figure 8.12.

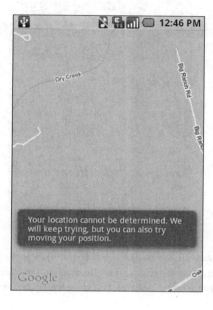

Figure 8.12
Sometimes, even your phone has no idea where you are.

But we're getting ahead of ourselves. We'll talk much more about GPS in the section "Using Google Maps with GPS." For now, let's start with some of the basics of viewing and using maps on your phone.

Viewing a Map

Your location on the map is marked with a flashing blue dot. Hopefully the phone has found your location easily and it's mostly correct. Now let's look at a few different views for your map. Press the Menu button and then tap Map mode to display the screen shown in Figure 8.13.

Map View

The default map view is a road map. Tap Map on the Map mode menu if you've somehow gotten yourself into another map view.

As you're looking at the road map view, you can move around and zoom in and out. If you touch the screen, you get the same zoom in and out buttons that you get from the web browser. You can also drag the screen in whichever direction you want to move the map around, or use the trackball to move the map around.

Figure 8.13
Change the view of your map with the tap of a finger.

Although the default map view is a road map, you should never use your phone and the Map application while driving. Either have someone else in the car navigate, or pull over and check your map. Driving while dividing your attention between the road and that small screen is dangerous and, in many states, illegal.

The phone attempts to figure out where you are based on mobile phone towers. The result looks something like what you see in Figure 8.14.

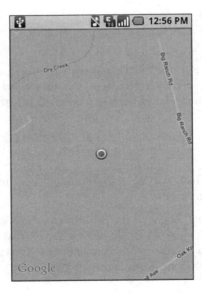

Figure 8.14
Where in the world (more or less) are the authors?

As you can see, the dot shows approximately where we are currently located. The first person to email us and tell us where we are—well, who knows? Maybe we'll send you an auto-graphed copy of the book (assuming you even want a second copy). If you scroll around a lit-tle bit, you'll also notice a circle surrounding that glowing dot. The circle doesn't serve much purpose other than to show all portions of the map within half a mile of your current location.

When the phone approximates your location from mobile phone towers, as opposed to GPS, you should really put emphasis on the word "approximate." If you live in an urban environ-ment and have a good signal from all the local towers, you might be close to the dot. However, don't believe what you see on *Law & Order* and *CSI* about being able to track exactly where someone is as he or she walks down the street.

In fact, if you just leave the map up, it may refresh itself and believe you're in a completely dif-ferent location without your even moving, all through the magic of triangulation.

You might notice that the map showing the failure (Figure 8.12) and the map showing where you are (Figure 8.14) are the same. When you start the map, it should start with where you were last according to the map, even after a reboot of the phone.

The road map is pretty cool, but several other views offer even more information, as discussed in the following sections. Press Menu and tap Map mode again, and then tap Traffic.

Traffic View

Traffic reports have always confused me. Sometimes I'm already in the middle of wherever the traffic is, and thus too late to avoid it. Or maybe there is only one route to wherever I want to go, so it's impossible to avoid. Other times the alternative route is far enough out of the way that taking it wouldn't save me any time.

The map, however, comes with a handy Traffic feature.

Simply press the Menu button, tap Map mode, and then tap Traffic. If you're lucky enough to live in an area with online traffic information available, you see something like Figure 8.15.

If you don't see the telltale green, yellow, and red highlights on the roads, you might not live in an area that has online traffic information available. More and more areas are providing traffic information, so if you don't see traffic information today, don't despair. You might find it in six months or so.

The Traffic view screen can be very helpful when you're away from your computer and need to know the fastest way to get from point A to point B. We use it all the time to check traffic between our house and the airport or between work and home. You can even use it to find the quickest way home after a late-night concert.

Figure 8.15
You can't see it in this black-and-white figure, but green, yellow, and red highlights tell you where the traffic is and where things are moving along just fine.

A very simple way to tell whether traffic information is available in your area is to head to your computer and surf to http://maps.google.com. Click the Traffic link at the top of the map. If you zoom out to see the United States, you see traffic lights in every area where you can get traffic information, as shown in Figure 8.16. Click one of the traffic lights, and then click the Zoom In link.

Figure 8.16
If only there were that few traffic lights in the world!

Satellite View

Road and Traffic maps are handy, but sometimes you want to see an aerial view of where you are.

Press the Menu button, tap Map mode, and tap Satellite; you see something like what is shown in Figure 8.17. As with the Street view, you can zoom in and out. Just don't expect to be able to read license plates or check out the color of someone's eyes.

Figure 8.17
Hey, that's my house!

Looking at the aerial view of your house, and someone else's car is in the driveway? Is your house a color it hasn't been in two years? Is your relatively new office building not even there? Well, aerial view isn't an actual live satellite view. It's a compilation of static images taken at some past date.

Although the satellite maps are good for a wow factor, they usually are helpful only when you need a landmark while driving around. But you can see landmarks with Street view too, as you'll read next.

As mentioned previously, never use your phone while driving. Pull over and check your phone while your car is parked.

Street View

First, the bad news: Street view is available in only certain areas. Some are obvious, like the Bay Area in Northern California, Seattle, and New York City. Others are not so obvious, like Mount Shasta National Park in Northern California. But where Street view is available, it can be a great way to figure out where something is.

To see where Street view is available, go to http://maps.google.com/help/maps/streetview/ in your web browser on your computer. You should see most locations that are available in Street view.

You have a more advanced method of finding what is available in street view. Go to http://maps.google.com. At the top of the zoom bar on the left stands the Google street view "man." Click and drag him onto the map of the United States. Areas with Street view are blue on the map.

Now, the good news: If you live in an area covered by Street view, you can see it on your phone.

Start by pressing the Menu button and tapping Map mode and then tapping Street view.

If you're covered by Street view, or at least the area you're looking at on the map is, the roads are outlined in blue, as shown in Figure 8.18.

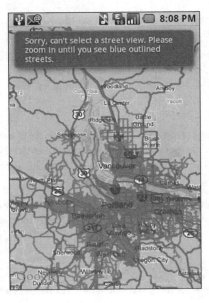

Figure 8.18
If this were in color, you could see the blue.

Normally, when you want to see the Street view, you just tap the blue road you want to see. As you can see in Figure 8.18, we aren't zoomed in quite enough to get Street view to work; we need to zoom in quite a bit to be able to use it. For now, just tap the plus sign to zoom in.

After you are fully zoomed in, indicated by the fact that the zoom in button is now unusable, you should be able to tap a road. If you find it difficult to tap a road you want, you can use the trackball to move the small circle around the screen, stopping it on the road you want. After you've tapped where you want, or anywhere near a Street view location, a little box shows you what you've selected, as shown in Figure 8.19. You also might see a little snapshot of where you're looking.

Figure 8.19
A sneak preview of what Street view shows you.

If this is the location you want to see, tap the box. You see something like Figure 8.20.

Figure 8.20
Driving down the street, virtually.

The screen shows a gray line stretching off into the distance, along with two arrows—one pointing toward you and one pointing away. Tapping either of these moves you in that direction. Moving your finger around the screen allows you to look around.

If you press the Menu button, you can also step forward and back, as well as zoom in on any image. Note that when you zoom in, you can move forward and backward only by using the Menu, not the screen. When you do move, you zoom right back out.

As with the Satellite view, Street view is a compilation of images taken at a fixed point in time. It can be fun to walk through street view and see the weather change from sunny to cloudy. All this means is that the part of the street that's sunny was recorded on a different day than the part of the street that's cloudy.

Two other options show up when you press the Menu button. The first is Report image. Tapping this opens a web browser so that you can report an image, as shown in Figure 8.21. You can report Privacy Concerns, such as removing your house, or blurring out someone's face or a license plate. Inappropriate Content covers nudity and the like. The general Other option covers blurry images, incorrect images, security concerns, and so on.

Figure 8.21

If you see something inappropriate, report it.

The second option is Compass mode. If you just tap it, you won't see what's so cool about it. You need to pick up your phone, hold it in front of your eyes, and then spin.

If you look at the Street view of where you are right now, the phone recognizes what direction you are facing. As you turn, the phone moves the picture to show you what you should be seeing.

Searching for a Location

You can move your way around the map with your finger only so quickly, and accuracy obviously is an issue. There must be an easier way to find things, right? Enter the Search box.

Press the Menu button and tap Search. You see a simple text box where you can type in a location you'd like to find.

When you open the Search box, you see a list of things you've searched for before, including My Location. I happen to be fond of the restaurant Cha Cha Lounge in Los Angeles, so I'll type cha cha lounge, los angeles, ca. You don't always need to be so precise. If a place is uniquely named and in your local area, you can leave off the city and state, and you likely will find it. If you know the address, you can search for that.

After you type in what you want to search for, either tap the Search button on the screen or press Enter, and you see a list. Tap the item in the list you want to see; you get something like what is shown in Figure 8.22. If you tap the Show map button, you go to the first item in the list. Tapping Edit search takes you back to the search box.

Figure 8.22
They have the best jerk pork.

You have a couple options on this screen. First, the left and right arrows next to the name and address you searched for move you through the list of items that came up in the search.

The lower-right corner of the screen has a button that allows you to return to your search results.

Last, the map is populated with numerous pushpins, each of which represents a different item from the search box. You can tap a pushpin to jump to its location.

If you tap the box containing the address you're looking at, you're given a few options of what to do. You can zoom in to the address so that you get a close-up of the area. If you searched for a business name and the phone number is listed, you can call the business with a simple tap. We'll skip the directions option for now, because we'll talk about that in a moment. You also have the option to add this business as a contact so that you can find it more easily. Also, if the business has a website in Google's directories, you have a very simple method to visit it.

Using Google Maps with GPS

One of the better features of modern phones is the convenience of having a built-in GPS, removing the need for you to carry a separate device.

Don't get me wrong. A dedicated GPS device has more features when it comes to getting from here to there, but your phone's GPS capabilities are a good substitute.

To use the GPS, first you must turn it on.

But before you do that, you need to know that GPS drains your battery. If at all possible, keep the phone plugged into a charger while you use the GPS. If you need to use the GPS while not on a charger, make sure you disable the GPS when you're finished using it.

To turn on the GPS, tap the Application tab, tap Settings, tap Security & location, and tap Enable GPS satellites.

That's all you have to do to enable it.

Note that GPS probably won't work while you're inside a building.

Getting Directions

You just read about one way to get directions to (or from) a location. How about another? When you're looking at a map, press the Menu button and tap Directions to get something much like what is shown in Figure 8.23.

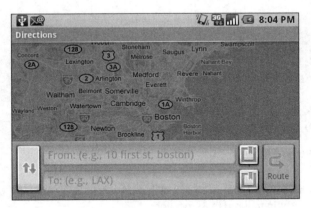

Figure 8.23
A man's worst enemy: getting directions from a map.

You'll find that you can get to a certain level of vagueness in your directions. For instance, you can simply put in a city and state for your starting location, and the directions you are given start from the center of the city you've selected. This is an excellent workaround for when you know the basics of how to get out of town, but not the specifics of how to get where you're going. We all know that online directions are not always the best when it comes to the ins and outs of a city, but generally they are correct. So, to save time, rather than starting from your home address, just start from your city. You know how to get to the highway, after all, and you probably know a better way than the directions will give you.

Also, if you don't know the address of where you are going, and it's a business, you can put in the same sort of information you'd have used in a search to find it on the map.

So, when I'm in Boston, and I want to find a way to get to Bob's Clam Hut in Kittery, Maine (not that I need directions; I'm pretty good at getting there blindfolded), I can just start at Boston, MA, and end at Bob's Clam Hut, Kittery, ME, and tap Route.

Do not attempt to drive blindfolded.

But let's make a pit stop here, because the directions search screen has a few other interesting features. The button on the left, for instance, swaps the Start and End locations.

Also, the buttons to the right of the start and end locations allow you to fill the box with an address you've used before, the address of one of your contacts, or your current location. This is an exceedingly useful option if you have the GPS enabled.

After you put in your start and end location and tap the Route button, you see a list of directions, much like what is shown in Figure 8.24.

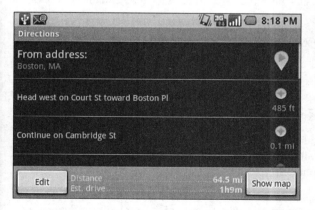

Figure 8.24
You actually can get there from here.

From the list of directions, you have a couple different options.

First, you can tap the Show map button. This takes you to the start of the route, as shown in Figure 8.25.

On this screen, you can tap the location, or the right arrow, to move to the next step in the directions. After you've moved past the first step, you can tap the left arrow to go back to the previous step if necessary.

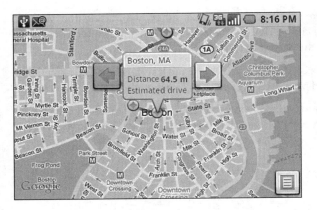

Figure 8.25
No, really, you can get there.

In the lower right is a button that takes you back to the list of directions.

From the directions screen you can also tap any particular step to zoom to that part of the map. This is really good when you know how to get halfway there, so you need directions after only a certain point.

The directions have some drawbacks. First, unlike a normal GPS, the phone's GPS doesn't tell you when you're off course, or readjust your directions based on going off course.

Also, as you approach a waypoint, the map doesn't update to where you are; nor can you see the directions and the map at the same time. You can only view the map and tap on a single step of the directions at once.

If you have a navigator riding with you, the GPS works great. If you're driving alone, it's not quite as useful.

Other Google Applications

It might seem like we've covered quite a bit of features that Google offers, but we've only scratched the surface. Google has an entire suite of applications that have been specifically designed to be used on a mobile phone.

Well, that's not entirely true. These applications were written without mobile phones in mind; they were created for general use on computers. But because of the applications' popularity, special mobile-friendly versions were created just for mobile phones. And following that were special versions for mobile phones with touch screens.

To see the touch-friendly applications, just fire up your web browser and tap the More link at the top, or look at Figure 8.26. We'll focus on a couple that you might enjoy or at least find very useful.

Figure 8.26
Google mobile applications.

Google Reader

Google Reader is an easy way to keep up with the blogs that interest you. No matter what computer you're using, when you mark something as read, it will be marked as read everywhere.

If you're used to using the web-based reader, I highly recommend trying out the mobile phone version on your Android-powered phone. The touch-based interface is very intuitive and easy to use.

If you've never used the web-based reader, on your computer go to http://www.google.com/reader. From here you can add new RSS feeds and even organize your feeds into groups.

To set up Google Reader and subscribe to feeds, you need to use your computer. You cannot subscribe to feeds from your phone.

After you've subscribed to a blog (or two, or three, or fifty), open the browser on your phone. While you're looking at the Google search page, tap the Reader link at the top of the screen. You see all the unread items , as shown in Figure 8.27.

This view is good if you follow a small group of blogs. But if you follow too many and prefer to read them blog by blog, tap Feeds to see your subscribed blogs, rather than all the individual posts. Figure 8.28 shows what we mean.

Figure 8.27
Way too much to read.

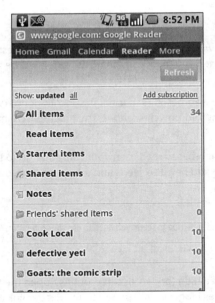

Figure 8.28
Still too much to read.

Just tap a blog's name to see a list of items that are currently unread from that blog. Tap the individual item to open and read it.

Google Docs

Google Docs, at http://docs.google.com, is an online competitor to Microsoft Office, OpenOffice, and the other desktop office-type applications. Google Docs lets you create spreadsheets, documents, and presentations and store them online so that you can access them anywhere. Also you can share those documents with other people using Google Docs for collaboration purposes.

The downside is that you can't actually create documents on your phone; you can only read them.

The upside is that you can read documents on your phone, without having to copy them to your phone, just by loading Google Docs.

To get to the docs, in the browser tap More, and then tap Docs. If you weren't already on the Google search page, just go to www.google.com by pressing the Menu button and tapping Go to URL.

If you've created some documents, spreadsheets, and so on, you see a screen like the one shown in Figure 8.29.

Figure 8.29

A virtual filing cabinet.

Tap the item you want to open. As you can see from the last item in the list, some items might be shared. Suppose you're working in a collaborative environment, and you want to see only the things you've created. You can tap Owned By Me at the top to see only your things, rather than everything you've gotten invitations to work with too.

Perhaps a future version will allow you to actually edit the files, but for now, you'll have to be satisfied with just reading.

Adding New Applications

Your phone can do some wonderful things, and we've talked about many of them. But we'll be honest. It can't do everything.

It can't tell you what song is playing when you hold up the phone. It can't tell you how much that book you're holding costs at a number of websites and local stores. It can't adjust its ringtone or volume based on where you are.

But what if it could?

Enter the Market.

Some of those things you wish your phone could do might be possible. Someone who wants the same functionality that you do and who writes computer software, might have written a program, and the Market is where you go to get those programs.

Tap the Application tab, and then tap Market. You see the Market screen, as shown in Figure 9.1.

Figure 9.1
The Android Market: All that and a bag of chips.

Finding and Installing New Applications

Finding applications is easy. After you open the Market, you have a couple different options. First, at the top of the screen, you have some Featured pieces of software you can install. You can drag the featured applications left or right to scroll through them.

To check out a featured application, just tap it. You see a description of and comments about the software. Even though the featured applications are pretty interesting, maybe it's better to dive into the Applications option by tapping it. You see a list of categories, as shown in Figure 9.2.

As an example, let's install an application so that you can see how it works.

There's a cool little application we like where, while you're shopping, you can take a picture of a bar code and—well, why don't we just show you? Scroll down and tap Shopping. Your screen might not look like what you see in Figure 9.3, but you get the idea.

All the lists look like this, so now is a good time to note what you see. You have the option to see applications listed by popularity (number of downloads) or by date.

Figure 9.2
More categories than you can shake a large stick at.

Figure 9.3
The Shopping applications.

Speaking of those applications, let's focus in and point out what's here (see Figure 9.4).

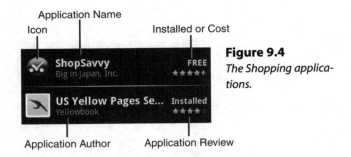

Figure 9.4

The Shopping applications.

First and foremost is the icon. This is what it will look like on the Application tab. Although you shouldn't judge an application by its icon, I've seen my fair share of ugly icons. Unlike on your computer, you can't change icons on your phone.

Next to that are the application's name and author, which might be a person or a company. You also see a notation about whether the application is installed and whether it has a cost. Below that is a rating of the application by other people who have downloaded and installed it.

Now that you know all that, tap ShopSavvy so that you can review what the application does and install it.

The application's page shows you some basic information, giving you the ability to Rate it! (which is something you should do for applications you like, or that you want to warn people away from). You also can read other people's comments about the application.

As the description says, this application scans bar codes and then looks up prices of the product, not just online but at local stores. Cool, huh?

If you like the application and want to see if the people who made it have made any other applications, that's another thing you can do from here.

Tap the Install button. You see the warning shown in Figure 9.5.

This application needs to be able to do a few things with your phone in order to operate. It needs to be able to take pictures, it needs to be able to figure out where you are, and it needs to connect to the Internet to look up prices. If you just don't feel comfortable letting the application do all this, tap Cancel. However, we feel pretty confident that this application is legitimate and won't do anything untoward with our phone, so we'll tap OK.

You see an icon on the Notification bar while the software is downloading and installing, as shown in Figure 9.6. When it's done, you see a different icon, as shown in Figure 9.7.

Figure 9.5
Scarier than a sky of flying monkeys, or maybe just a field of poppies.

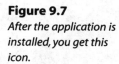

Figure 9.6
This icon in the notification area tells you that you're downloading an application.

Figure 9.7
After the application is installed, you get this icon.

Press the Home button, tap the Application tab, find ShopSavvy, and tap it to start the application.

Using ShopSavvy

After you've loaded ShopSavvy, as shown in Figure 9.8, to search for any product you have in front of you, just tap Search for a product to display the screen shown in Figure 9.9.

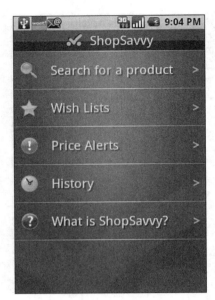

Figure 9.8
Use ShopSavvy whenever you shop.

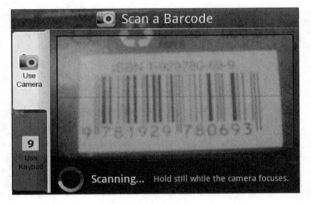

Figure 9.9
Scan any bar code to begin searching.

Position your phone with the camera facing the bar code of the item you're interested in. Just hold the phone steady. You might need to move the phone closer to or farther from the bar code until it comes into focus. You don't have to click anything on the phone; the software takes care of everything for you. When the software has successfully scanned the bar code, it searches for the item. After it finds the item, it displays the screen shown in Figure 9.10.

To see where you can buy this item, just tap either Web or Local. In our case, tapping Web produces the results shown in Figure 9.11.

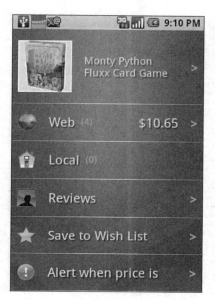

Figure 9.10
You can find this item at a variety of stores, both online and local.

Figure 9.11
A variety of stores and a variety of prices.

Now that you know where you can buy the item, and for what price, just tap the result you're interested in. From here, you can either go directly to the store's website (if one's available) or email a link to yourself or to anyone else who might be interested. Emailing a link produces an email message much like the one shown in Figure 9.12.

Figure 9.12
Look at this great price I found!

Not only can you see a list of stores that carry this item, but you also can read reviews of the item, save it to your wish list, and even set up an alert when the price drops below a certain price. To configure a price alert, tap Alert when price is to display the screen shown in Figure 9.13.

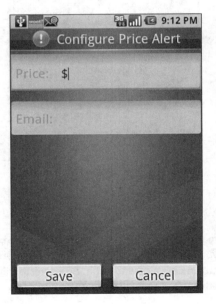

Figure 9.13
I want to know when that card game goes on sale.

Enter the price and your email address, and tap Save.

Have you ever gone into a bookstore and knew there were books you wanted, but you couldn't remember which ones? Well, wish lists can help you keep organized and never forget that book you wanted to buy. Tap Wish Lists on the ShopSavvy screen, and then press the Menu button and tap New to create a new wish list. Name your wish list, and then tap OK. Now you can scan any product you want and add it to your wish list.

The programs you can add to the phone aren't all business; there are some fun and games too.

Go back to the main page of Market and tap Games. You see a screen similar to Figure 9.14.

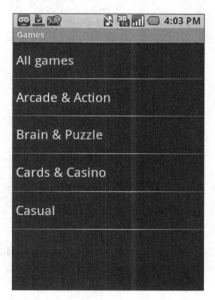

Figure 9.14
Gaming options abound.

Installing a game is the same as installing any other application, so we won't dive deeply into how to install a game. I recommend trying out Bonsai Blast or Coloroid just to see what sorts of games are out there. Games are a lot more fun to learn on your own, so we won't waste your time with instructions for Bonsai Blast. However, there are lots of fun applications out there that aren't technically games. Right now we'll play around with Shazam.

Using Shazam

Picture this scenario: You're out and about, in a store with ShopSavvy at your side, and a song comes at you over the air. Your toes start tapping, your hips start moving, and you decide to load Amazon MP3 from your phone and purchase the song. The only problem is that you don't know the song's name.

Enter Shazam. Just tap the application to launch it, and then tap Tag Now.

We're assuming, of course, that the song is still playing.

Shazam listens for a few moments and then analyzes what it's heard. When it finds a match (and it usually does), you see the screen shown in Figure 9.15.

Figure 9.15
The results of Shazam's search.

After Shazam has found the song, you can tap Search Amazon MP3 to immediately search for the song and purchase it, as shown in Figure 9.16.

Figure 9.16
Now you can enjoy the song anytime.

You can also search YouTube for clips that feature the song, as shown in Figure 9.17.

Figure 9.17
Search for YouTube clips that feature the song you just heard.

Managing Your Applications

Whatever application you install, there are some common tips and tricks that we think you should know. First, if you like an application and think you'll use it often, you can move it to the phone's desktop so that it is more easily accessible. Just follow these steps:

1. Slide the desktop to where you'd like the icon to live. Remember, your phone's desktop has three screens—the clock in the center, and a whole second and third screen to the right and left.

2. Open the **Application** tab, and tap and hold the icon you'd like to see on your desktop.

3. When the phone vibrates, the Application tab disappears and allows you to drop the icon wherever you wish.

If you want to remove an icon, tap and hold it. The Application tab turns red and changes to a trash can. Just drag the icon to the trash can, and it's gone.

Second, the Menu button is your friend. If you can't figure something out, try pressing the Menu button to see what options might be there to help you out.

Third, some things, such as items in a list, react to being tapped and held. So, when you are experimenting with different applications, be sure to give that method a try.

Adding Applications to Your Home Screen

Chapter 1, "The Phone Basics," showed you how to customize your home screen a bit. You can add shortcuts to the applications you've installed on your home screen.

One way to do this is to drag icons to your home screen, as discussed in the preceding section. But there's another method. First, tap and hold anywhere on the home screen (that's not an application) and select Application from the pop-up menu. Every application you have on your phone is listed here, as shown in Figure 9.18.

Figure 9.18
Did I really install all that?

Tap the icon you'd like to add. It shows up where you tapped and held the screen. If that's not where you want it, tap and hold the icon and drag it where you want it. If you want it on a different screen, you need to delete the icon and switch to the screen you want it on.

As a review, to delete the icon, just tap and hold the icon until the phone vibrates, and drag it to the Application tab, which should now have a little picture of a trash can. When you drag over it, it turns red. When you let go, no more icon.

Find More Applications Using Search

After you've spent some time going through the Applications and Games categories, you'll see that some things aren't in the category you expected them to be in.

This brings us to the Search function. You can get to Search either directly, on the main screen of the Market, or by pressing the Menu button on any screen within the Market and tapping

Search. Type in your search term, and press the Enter key on the keyboard or tap the Search button.

Search looks for the name, publisher, and description of the application, so try to keep your searches focused, rather than general.

Because the phone is an MP3 player as well as a phone, we'll search for an application that can help you when you're traveling in another country. Typing Spanish gives you the result shown in Figure 9.19.

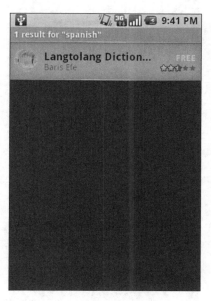

Figure 9.19

I need a Spanish-English translator.

Tap any of the results to display the information about the application. From here you can choose to install it or press the Back button to search again.

Uninstalling Unwanted Applications

Not every application is worthwhile for every person. I really like Shazam, but you might not, and that's okay.

So you want to get rid of it. That's easy enough:

1. From anywhere in the Market, press the **Menu** button.

2. Tap **My downloads**.

3. Tap the program you'd like to remove.

4. Tap the **Uninstall** button. You see the screen shown in Figure 9.20.

Figure 9.20
Are you sure?

5. If you're sure, click **OK**. You're asked why you want to remove the application, as shown in Figure 9.21.

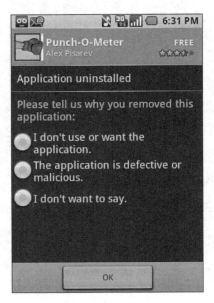

Figure 9.21
Share why you are unin-stalling.

6. If you added the icon to your desktop, you need to manually remove it. Tap and hold it until the Application tab turns into a trash can, and then drag the icon to the trash can.

It's important to share why you're uninstalling an application. This feedback does make it back to the application developer, who can use this information to make the application better.

You'll find that you can install tons of applications, and more are added all the time. Be sure to rate the applications you download so that others can learn from your opinions. Leave comments on the applications so that the developers can hear your feedback. Your phone has a limited amount of memory for applications, but we've installed 10 to 15 applications so far and haven't found a limit yet.

If you find anything really cool, email us. We'd love to see it too.

Using Wi-Fi

Your phone has a connection to the Internet almost everywhere you go. That's one of the benefits of having a mobile phone.

But "almost everywhere" is not the same as "everywhere," and that can be a problem.

Sometimes, you might be at work and, although you can get phone calls just fine, Internet service isn't very strong. That happens all the time where I work. Or maybe you're in an area with spotty service, and you need to check your email. Or possibly you're just running out of data in your data plan.

We recommend always purchasing an unlimited data plan with an Android-powered phone. Too many features use the Internet. Unless you plan to use Wi-Fi only to connect to the Internet, purchasing a restricted data plan can end up being very expensive if you exceed your download allowance.

Luckily, your phone lets you connect to a wireless network, like they have in coffee shops, libraries, schools, workplaces, and sometimes even bars!

If you don't have a wireless connection available, you might not be able to walk through these steps, so we'll provide a few extra figures so that you can see what's happening.

Setting Up Wi-Fi

First, tap the Applications tab, tap Settings, and tap Wireless controls. You see the settings shown in Figure 10.1.

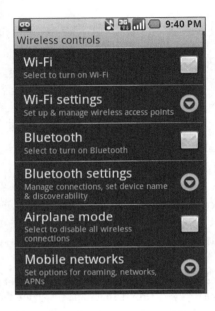

Figure 10.1
Wireless controls.

Although you can turn on Wi-Fi from here, you can do that from the Wi-Fi settings as well, so tap Wi-Fi settings.

Without Wi-Fi enabled, the only thing you can do here is enable Wi-Fi, so the next step is to tap that option.

Wi-Fi drains the battery pretty quickly. If you don't need it enabled, it's worth disabling. If you do need it enabled, it is wise to keep your phone plugged in.

As soon as Wi-Fi is enabled, your phone begins scanning for Wi-Fi networks. If any are available, you see them so that you can connect to them, as shown in Figure 10.2. If no networks are available, your phone scans for newly available networks on a regular schedule (every few minutes).

Note that open networks and secured networks are distinguished by an icon and a description. The network's relative strength is indicated by the white waves radiating from the dot. The more white, the better.

Figure 10.2
Enabled Wi-Fi.

If you want to force the phone to scan for a new network (perhaps because the network was temporarily unavailable when the phone last scanned), press the Menu button and tap Scan.

As you can see, two networks are available to connect to—one secured and one open.

A secured network requires a password or key to connect to it. An open network lets anyone connect to it. Lots of open public networks are available, particularly in large metropolitan areas. If you're in a location that you know offers free Wi-Fi, feel free to connect to an open network. However, all data that you send to the Internet through this open network (including passwords and credit card numbers) could potentially be monitored by the network's owner. Although this isn't common, it can definitely happen. Certain coffee shops and bookstores often have secured networks because they require you to purchase some of their product before you can use their wireless networks.

We cannot condone stealing Wi-Fi from someone's house or business that isn't intending to offer their Wi-Fi free. We also recommend that if you have a wireless network at home, be sure to secure it.

When you attempt to connect to an open network, you see the signal strength and security of the network you're connecting to, as shown in Figure 10.3.

Figure 10.3
Connecting to an open network.

If you connect to a secured network, you see something like what is shown in Figure 10.4.

Figure 10.4
Connecting to a secured network.

You need to use the keyboard to type in the security code. If you're like me, you'll want to check the Show password box so that, instead of seeing dots, you'll be able read what you type. If you're connecting to a secured network in a public location, such as a coffee shop or an airport, you'll likely need to purchase access to the network. When you do so, you'll obtain the security code for the network. If you're connecting to a secured network that a friend owns, they will have to give you the security code.

You have a couple other options. First, there's the option to add a Wi-Fi network manually. Tap Add a Wi-Fi network to display the screen shown in Figure 10.5.

Figure 10.5
Creating your own wireless network connection.

You won't usually need to add a Wi-Fi connection manually. Your phone should automatically detect any available connection in range. However, suppose, for example, that you're going to a conference and you know secured Wi-Fi will be available. If you have the SSID (the network's code) and security information, you can actually set up the network ahead of time.

Occasionally, to connect to a network, you need to create the network on your device, be it phone or computer, before you can connect to it. You need to talk to whoever runs the wireless network to get the login credentials.

You also see advanced options after pressing the Menu button and tapping Advanced, as shown in Figure 10.6.

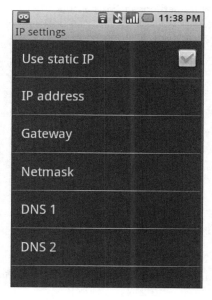

Figure 10.6
Custom IP address configuration.

This is another instance where you need to talk to whoever is running your wireless network. If you know what all this means, you probably know what values you need to provide. If you don't, you'll have to ask to find out.

As soon as you're connected to a Wi-Fi network, your Internet traffic is routed over that network rather than over your mobile phone's data plan.

Other Wireless Options

While we're talking about wireless and looking at the wireless controls (shown back in Figure 10.1), we should mention a few other options.

Bluetooth is a technology developed to allow computer devices to speak to each other over short distances, such as within a single room.

One of the more common uses of Bluetooth is earpieces for mobile phones. You've probably seen people wearing them, walking down the street, appearing to talk to themselves while they look you in the eye. These earpieces are also becoming the norm in states where using a mobile phone while driving is illegal and use of hands-free headsets is the law. Another common use is in Wii and Xbox 360 controllers, which use Bluetooth for communications between the controller and the console.

Enabling Bluetooth

Just like with Wi-Fi, you can turn on Bluetooth from either the main list of wireless controls or from Settings, so let's look at the settings shown in Figure 10.7.

Figure 10.7
Bluetooth options.

You have three basic options here:

- **Bluetooth:** This option enables or disables Bluetooth.
- **Discoverable:** If you would like other devices to be able to find this device, you need to check this option.
- **Device name:** When your phone is discoverable, it shows a name. By default, it's a pretty plain name. If you tap the Device name, you can change it to whatever you want.

After you've enabled Bluetooth and have a device you'd like to connect to it, press the Menu button and tap Scan for devices. When you see the device you want to connect, or pair, to, tap it. That's all you need to do, unless the remote device is protected, in which case you need to type in a PIN.

Airplane Mode

Although there's consistent talk about airlines allowing mobile phone use on airplanes, this hasn't happened yet. So if you want to use your phone on a plane, you need to check Airplane mode. You won't be able to use the Internet, but you'll be able to do anything that is on your phone and that doesn't require any form of wireless connectivity, such as listening to music.

The Professor and Mary Ann: Mobile Networks

Just like the original theme song relegated the Professor and Mary Ann to "and the rest" on *Gilligan's Island*, I'll leave the Mobile networks section to a more advanced book. By and large, these settings are not for a normal user, although your mobile phone provider's technical support may have you go into these settings to test certain things.

The only option of any interest to the average user under these settings is the ability to shut off data when your phone is in roaming mode. Some mobile phone providers charge an arm and a leg for data connections while you're roaming. This can happen if you're in an area where your mobile phone service is very weak or if you're traveling outside your home country. You should talk to your mobile phone service provider and find out if they charge more for data if you're roaming. If they do, you may want to uncheck this option. It could save you a pretty penny.

If you want to use your phone to browse the Internet when you're in a foreign country, try using Wi-Fi instead of your cellular data connection. Many cities these days have free Wi-Fi somewhere, either in restaurants, coffee shops, or even some hotels. Just be sure to shut off Wi-Fi when you're done to conserve the battery.

Security

Whenever you use your phone for more than just ordering pizza, you're storing at least a little sensitive information on it. Whether it's just your mother's phone number or the keycodes for the entire kingdom, you'll want to protect your data.

SIM Card Lock

This extra bit of security allows you to lock your phone's SIM card (the little card that lets you connect to your mobile phone provider). That way, no one can make phone calls without the PIN.

If you'd like to set this up, tap the Application tab, tap Settings, tap Security & location, and then tap SIM card lock.

The settings are rather basic:

- Enable Lock SIM card locks the SIM card.
- Change PIN code changes the PIN code.

Don't you wish everything was so clearly labeled?

If you don't know your SIM card PIN, you need to contact your mobile phone service provider. You can't lock your SIM card without that PIN.

You'll still be able to make emergency calls (such as 911 in the United States).

Locking your SIM card won't prevent anyone from accessing documents stored on your phone, so don't rely on it to secure all your data. If you're worried about someone accessing your data when you're not in possession of your phone, use the screen lock function, discussed next.

Screen Lock

The G1 phone from T-Mobile (as well as many other Android-powered phones) has a rudimentary form of screen time-out that kicks in whenever the phone hasn't been used for a minute or so. To turn the screen back on, you have to press the red Hang Up button and then press the Menu button. All this feature does is prevent your phone from accidentally dialing someone while it's in your pocket. If you want to secure your phone further, use the phone's screen lock feature. Your phone has a lot of important data on it. If you should happen to lose it, you don't want people to be able to easily access that data.

With the touch screen being such a major part of this phone, there's an ingenious method of unlocking the phone that lets your fingers do the walking—or, in this case, sliding.

Tap the Application tab, tap Settings, and tap Security & location. We'll focus on the Screen unlock portion of the list.

First you need to set an unlock pattern, so tap that option. You see an information screen explaining what you need to do, followed by a screen that looks something like Figure 11.1.

As the instructional page said, you need to draw a pattern on the screen, connecting the dots. You need to drag through at least four dots; they don't need to be adjacent. For example, although it is extremely tricky to create, Figure 11.2 is an allowed pattern. If you have small fingers, you might be better able to create a complex pattern.

After you've input the pattern once, you're asked to verify the pattern by doing it again. As soon as all the verifying and confirming are done, you can choose whether to require the pattern to unlock the phone. If you don't, the device is always open.

If you choose to use the pattern, you can choose another option as well. The Use visible pattern option displays feedback on the screen as you're unlocking your phone. If you uncheck this option, you don't see the trail that your finger makes as you drag it across the screen. Unchecking this option will prevent anyone who looks over your shoulder from getting a good look at your pattern, but it can also make it harder to enter a complex pattern.

If it was at all tricky to make your pattern, you may not want to uncheck Use visible pattern. You may not be able to unlock your phone again, which leads us to the next section.

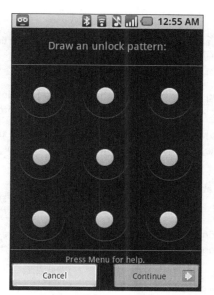

Figure 11.1
Let's play connect the dots!

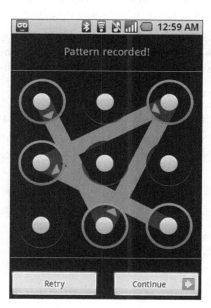

Figure 11.2
No exaggeration—this took 15 attempts to do.

Starting Over—Completely

For whatever reason, you want to start from scratch with your phone. Maybe you want to use a different Google account. Maybe you forgot your unlock pattern. Or maybe you just want to get rid of all your data, installed programs, settings, and customizations.

If you ever sell your phone, or give it to someone, be sure to follow the steps in this section. Otherwise, your data could end up where you least expect it, such as all over the Internet.

Starting over is easy enough to do, but reread that last sentence. Almost everything goes away. The only things that stay are files on the SD card, such as photographs and music files.

Well, and all your mail, contacts, and calendar information, because those are actually stored at Google and not on the phone. Regardless, starting over is a really big decision that shouldn't be taken lightly.

Now that you've thought about it, let's say you want to do it.

There are two ways, really.

If you can access your phone (in other words, you haven't forgotten your unlock code), you can just tap the Application tab, tap Settings, tap SD card & phone storage, and then tap Factory data reset.

But if you can't do that, follow these steps to reset:

1. Power off the phone by pressing the red **Hang Up** button.

2. After the device has powered down, hold down the **Home** key and press the red **Hang Up** button to start the phone. Keep holding down the buttons until you see the screen that shows a picture of the phone and the exclamation warning.

3. Slide open the keyboard and press **Alt+W**.

The phone should now reboot. It will be as if you just took it out of the box.

An Open-Source Platform

As we discussed in the Introduction, Android-powered phones are an open-source platform. It's easy to develop for an open-source platform (provided that you know some programming) because anyone can open and read the code. So when you're developing applications for your Android-powered phone, you can read the source code for the phone's software and build applications that work closely with the phone's software.

Not only is it easy to develop for the phone, but it's also easy to read the code behind the phone. Of course, although reading the code is easy, understanding it and being able to work with it aren't as easy.

Want to read the code? Head to http://source.android.com/ (on your computer). The link to get the source is on the main page.

Programming is a very advanced topic. You might not need or want to do anything like that with your phone. But if you do, we'd like to give you some pointers, as best we can.

Creating Applications for Your Phone

Right now, all programming for Android phones needs to be done in Java. If you don't program but have decided to read this chapter anyway, Java is more than just coffee or an island in the South Pacific. It's also a programming language that Sun Microsystems developed in the mid-1990s.

If you've never heard of Java, you may want to start with some basic Java information. Check out http://en.wikibooks.org/wiki/Java_Programming, http://en.wikiversity.org/wiki/Topic:Java, or http://forums.sun.com/index.jspa. You also might want to read *Sams Teach Yourself Java 6 in 21 Days*, 5th Edition.

But before we talk about installing the SDK, why don't we see if the following code scares you off? This is what your most basic application for Android looks like—the standard Hello World application:

```
package com.android.hello;

import android.app.Activity;
import android.os.Bundle;
import android.widget.TextView;

public class helloandroid extends Activity {
    /** Called when the activity is first created. */
    @Override
    public void onCreate(Bundle savedInstanceState) {
        super.onCreate(savedInstanceState);
        TextView tv = new TextView(this);
        tv.setText("Hello, Android");
        setContentView(tv);
    }
}
```

When you're learning a new programming language, a common first step is to create a program called Hello World. Its sole purpose is to print the phrase "Hello World" to the screen.

Let's go through the code and see what it does. If you're an experienced programmer, you can skip ahead to the next section.

The first line of the code, which begins with `package`, names and classifies your little program. A package is a way to organize Java classes into a namespace, which is just a fancy way of saying that it's a way to group similar things. Traditionally, a package is named hierarchically, going from most common to least common. It usually is named after the domain of whoever created the package. In this case, because the application was created by the good folks at Android, it's named `com.android`. If Android were located in the UK, this might be `uk.com.android`. The `hello` portion gives the package a specific name.

Next we tell the program what bits of information we need. We need to tell the system what we want to do, and we need to use the parts of the system that allow us to do those things. Think of it this way: In your brain, you have a little program for making coffee. It utilizes a few different parts of your brain: hand movement, measuring estimates, eyesight. That program for making coffee needs to be able to directly tell the hands what to do: scoop the coffee, drop it in the French press, and so on. For your "make coffee" program to work, you tell it that it needs to import the `me.hands` portion of your own personal operating system. In the preceding code, we're telling the `android.hello` program that we'll be performing an activity, working with the OS, and displaying text.

The final section of the program is called a class module. A class module is a self-contained bit of code that contains an instruction (or instructions) for what the code will do. In programming terms, it includes property and method definitions. A property is something descriptive about an object, and a method is something the object does. You might go so far as to say that a property is a noun that can be described with an adjective (such as red hair), and a method is a verb (such as drive).

So what is our class module doing? Well, in a nutshell, it's calling the `TextView` method, which displays text on the phone. Then it sets that displayed text to be `Hello, Android`. That's it. You've just written (okay, copied from us) your first program.

Installing the SDK

Now that you're almost ready to code, let's look at installing the Software Development Kit, or, as it's known in the programming world, the SDK.

If you're a nonprogrammer who is reading this chapter to educate yourself, let's talk about what an SDK is. It isn't much unlike this book. It is just a set of instructions on how to program for something, be it Microsoft Word, Amazon's website, or your phone. An SDK contains tools, descriptions of the programming commands used to communicate with the system, and lots of purely technical and, if you're not ready for it, completely confusing documentation.

On your computer, go to http://code.google.com/android/download.html. You should see something like Figure 12.1.

Figure 12.1
End-user license agreements creep up everywhere.

If you agree to the license, which you probably should if you want to program, put a check in the box that says you agree to the terms of the SDK license, and then click the Continue button.

At this point, simply download the SDK package that is applicable to your computer, be it Windows, Macintosh, or Linux.

Technically speaking, Windows Vista is supported, but we've had issues with getting the SDK applications to run properly on the 64-bit version of Vista. And there may not be a device driver for the phone, so you won't be able to debug the application either. A device driver will likely be available in the future, but no 64-bit driver currently exists.

Google gives you some instructions on how to install the SDK at http://code.google.com/android/intro/installing.html.

As you can see there, you need to install an Integrated Development Environment (IDE), with Eclipse being the primary suggestion. Why Eclipse? That's what Google recommends as part of the installation procedure.

An IDE is a set of graphical tools that help you write software. Think of it as the difference between Notepad and Microsoft Word. You can write a letter in either, but Word gives you far more tools to make the letter prettier. Programming is like that. You can write software in a program like Notepad and then, using some tools, convert that text into a program that actually runs. Or you can use an IDE, where you can do everything all in one place.

I recommend installing Eclipse from www.eclipse.org/downloads, unless you have a Java development environment you prefer.

After you've installed Eclipse and the optional plug-in—wait. Optional plug-in? How do you know if you need that? Let's start with how you know if you *don't* need it. If you won't be using Eclipse, you won't need the plug-in for it. Otherwise, the Android Development Tools plug-in would help you work directly with the Android SDK and make things work a little faster and easier as you develop for the phone. So, again, after you've installed Eclipse and the optional plug-in, start Eclipse. Then I recommend going through the Hello World tutorial. If you don't see the Tutorial icon, or if it doesn't look like Figure 12.2 (and you're running Eclipse 3.4), select Help, Welcome. You may also need to click the Restore Welcome link at the top of the page. If you're familiar enough with programming, this is a good tutorial for learning the interface and how to start.

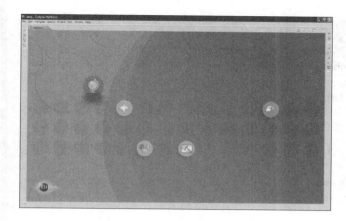

Figure 12.2
Your Eclipse might look like this, or it might not. Software changes fast.

If you're new to programming, I recommend checking out the websites and book I mentioned earlier.

After you've tried out the interface and tried the Hello World tutorial, my next recommendation is to head to http://code.google.com/android/intro/hello-android.html and walk through the Hello World example built especially for Android.

If you get the tutorial to work right, you'll see something like Figure 12.3.

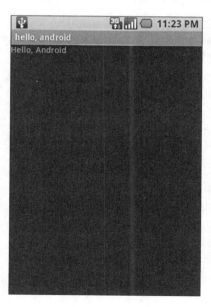

Figure 12.3
Hello, Android!

Don't want to use Eclipse? That's fair enough. You can do everything with the SDK tools that you installed in the first place outside the IDE environment; it just isn't as easy. Software gets created in a text-based editor. You need to install a compiler to make the text you type actual software that will run on the phone. I stick with an IDE. But if you're feeling brave, I'd definitely start by taking a look at http://code.google.com/android/intro/tools.html to gain a deeper understanding of the SDK and the included tools.

Resources

Programming is hard, and programming for a phone can be even harder. But you have a great community of people you can work with to help figure out the problems you're having and make your application go.

First and foremost, you'll want to go to http://code.google.com/android/groups.html. This is as official as an Android community can be, hosted at Google using its Groups forums for discussions.

http://androidcommunity.com/forums/ also has a couple development communities that you may want to review.

Currently these are the only two active forums. We're sure more will pop up as more people buy this phone and start writing applications for it. I recommend going to www.google.com and searching for "Android programming forums."

If you are looking for some forums where you can learn Java, you might want to start at http://forums.java.net or http://forums.sun.com.

Troubleshooting

Your phone is a complicated piece of equipment. Sure, it's small, and it appears relatively simple on the outside, but a lot of little things can go wrong. We don't want to scare you, though. Most of the problems you will encounter are pretty simple to resolve. This chapter covers a few of the basic problems you might encounter and helps you take some steps to fix them.

Service Issues

Mobile phones have come a long way in the past few years. It used to be that when I wanted to make a phone call from my house, I had to be next to my bedroom window, on a clear day, when the moon was in retrograde. Well, okay, it wasn't quite that bad, but I definitely couldn't walk around my whole house and expect to maintain a connection to whomever I was talking to.

Fast-forward a few years, and there are very few places where I can't make a call. However, very few isn't none. I still can't receive calls or reliably browse the Internet in my office at work due to very thick walls and a wealth of electronic equipment. And a tunnel I drive through occasionally doesn't have service either.

If you find that your phone disconnects from someone you're talking to, or you are trying to load a web page in the browser and it suddenly stops loading, the first place to look is at your phone's Notification bar, as shown in Figure 13.1.

Signal Strength

Figure 13.1
*The Notification bar
shows your antenna
strength.*

The little square with the four vertical bars shows your signal strength. If you have four bars, your signal strength is strong, and you shouldn't have any problem making calls or browsing the Internet. If you have only one bar (or no bars), you might not be able to make a call. Move to a different area, and see if your signal strength improves.

If you've gone outside, driven down the block, or even driven to a major city, and you just can't get more than one bar anywhere, contact your mobile service provider. Some service providers just don't have service in some areas. However, it is possible that there is a problem with the little card that activates your phone (the SIM card). Because this card is removable, your mobile service provider should be able to replace your SIM card with a new one to see if that fixes the problem.

So what can you do if your phone never gets a good signal at your house or office? Well, you've got three options. First, you can wait and see if your mobile phone company builds more towers in your area. Second, you can try canceling your service and switching to another company. If you're on a contract, though, and you're past the first 30 days, this will likely cost you some money. The third and easiest option is to investigate what is called a signal booster. A variety of these are available, as you'll find out if you do a web search for "cell phone signal booster."

Hardware and Software Issues

Anything can break. Even going back to the tin cans connected with string that you might have used as a child, problems happen. If the string broke, you couldn't hear the other person.

Technology is no different. As technology gets more advanced, often more individual components can have problems. Hardware issues can take several different forms.

My Phone Is Slower Than Molasses in January

If you've been using your phone for a while, you might notice that tapping an icon or pressing a button doesn't work as well as it used to. You might tap the Browser picture and have to wait a full minute for the browser to open. Or you might press the Home button while browsing the Internet and have to wait for what seems like forever to return to the home screen.

The most common reason for this is that a program on your phone isn't releasing resources properly. That sounds kind of complicated, so let's explore it a little bit.

Your phone has a limited amount of memory. Think of memory as a bowl of pebbles. Every time you use a program (such as Gmail or the browser), that program takes a handful of pebbles from the bowl and uses them to do things such as display text on the screen. Usually, when you close a program, it puts all those pebbles back in the bowl. However, sometimes the program holds onto those pebbles. If you have too many programs holding onto their pebbles, the bowl eventually will be nearly empty. If the bowl is nearly empty, any new program won't be able to grab enough pebbles to run well.

This problem has a couple of resolutions. The easiest solution is to simply reboot your phone. Rebooting is the technical term for turning the power off. To turn the power off on your G1 phone, press and hold the red Hang Up button until you see the screen shown in Figure 13.2.

Figure 13.2
Powering off the phone.

Tap Power off, and the phone shuts down. As soon as the phone has shut down completely, you can press the red Hang Up button to power the phone back on.

If this does not resolve the slow response time, a recently installed program probably is causing your phone to run slowly. Start with the last application you installed, and uninstall it. To uninstall an application, follow these steps:

1. Tap the **Application** tab, and then tap **Settings**.

2. Tap **Applications**.

3. Tap **Manage applications** to display a list of all currently installed applications.

4. Tap the most recently installed application to display a screen similar to the one shown in Figure 13.3.

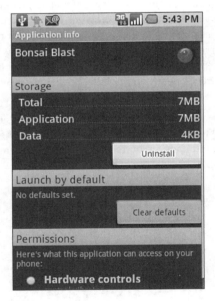

Figure 13.3
You can uninstall any custom application.

5. Tap the **Uninstall** button to uninstall your application.

6. Tap **OK** if you want to uninstall the application or **Cancel** if you've changed your mind.

After you uninstall one application, reboot the phone and see if the phone performs better. If not, uninstall the next most recently installed application, reboot, and try again. If, after uninstalling a handful of applications, your phone still isn't performing well, you might need to completely reset the phone. We'll cover that in just a bit.

My Phone Crashed

You were in the middle of a call, or you were playing a game or browsing the Internet, and all of a sudden the phone just shut down without warning. What's up with that? Well, there's no way to know for sure, but the most likely explanation is that a program running on the phone did something it wasn't supposed to. Often this happens when a program tries to tell the hardware to do something it can't do.

Unfortunately, there isn't much you can do about a crash other than just power the phone back on. As soon as the phone turns back on, try to repeat the action you were taking when the phone shut down. If it shuts down again, there is probably something wrong with the application you were using. In other words, you've probably encountered a bug. Either uninstall the application, or see if an update is available for it that fixes the problem.

If the phone keeps crashing when you do something simple like making a phone call or opening the Google home page in the browser, you might need to reset the phone.

My Phone Won't Do Anything

Are you pressing buttons and nothing's happening? Have you tried to call your mobile phone from a land line and it doesn't ring? What do you do?

Well, the simple answer is that you need to reboot your phone. Follow the steps provided in the previous sections to reboot your phone. If those instructions don't work, you'll have to remove the phone's back cover and then remove the battery. Leave the battery out of the phone for at least 30 seconds, and then reinsert the battery and replace the back cover. Power the phone back on again; everything should return to normal. If not, you might need to reset the phone.

I Dropped My Phone in Water

Take a random poll of your friends. Chances are, at least one of them has dropped his or her phone into some kind of liquid. Hopefully, the liquid was clean water, but we both know people who have dropped their phone in rather unmentionable places. I even know someone who left his phone in the pocket of a pair of shorts and *washed* and *dried* it!

So what do you do if your phone comes in contact with water? (If you dropped your phone into some other liquid, like a glass of soda, it's almost surely dead.) Well, there are no guarantees that these steps will work, but if you follow them, they will give you the best chance of being able to use your phone again:

1. Immediately remove your phone's back cover and battery.

2. Set the phone, battery, and cover on a dry, lint-free towel.

3. Do not touch the phone for three days.

4. Has it been three days? No? Don't touch the phone. Really.

5. Put the battery back in the phone, replace the cover, and try to power on the phone.

6. If the phone doesn't turn on, or behaves oddly, you can remove the battery again and leave the phone for another two days.

7. If, after the full five days, the phone still doesn't work, it probably never will.

Electronics don't respond well to water, and they do even worse if submerged in most any other liquid. However, unless your phone shorts out when it is dropped in the water, it is very possible that after the phone and all of its internal components dry completely, the phone will work just fine. We recommend three to five days of drying time. We've actually tested these steps (accidentally), and they did work. However, as they say, your mileage may vary.

It's a good idea to protect your phone from several different dangerous conditions. In addition to not dropping your phone (in or out of liquid), don't expose it to extreme temperatures for long periods of time. Leaving your phone in the car in 100-degree heat or sub-freezing temperatures for too long can cause irreparable damage.

Resetting Your Phone

Not to sound like a broken record, but if your phone crashes, or locks up (stops responding to anything you do), or just runs slower than you can stand, and the previous procedures don't fix the problems, you probably need to reset it. This should be used only as a last resort, because you will lose all installed applications and all custom data stored on the phone. Any information that you have stored in your Google account, such as your contacts and email, will still exist in your Google account, but you'll have to set up the phone again to synchronize that information to your phone.

To reset your phone, follow these steps:

1. Power off the phone by pressing the red **Hang Up** button.

2. After the device has powered down, hold down the **Home** key and press the red **Hang Up** button to restart the phone. Keep the keys held down until you have a screen that shows a picture of the phone and the exclamation warning.

3. Slide open the keyboard and press **Alt+W**.

The phone should reboot. It will be just like you took it out of the box.

If, after setting up your phone again, things still are not working correctly, contact technical support for your mobile provider. They might be able to replace or repair your phone.

Getting Help

If all else fails, there's always the Internet. Yes, the Internet is a wonderful, magical place where help abounds. No matter how smart you are (and I'm sure you are very smart), there is almost always someone on the Internet who is smarter than you. Or, at the very least, you'll find someone who knows more about your mobile phone than you do. These people are quite often very helpful and are happy to freely donate their time to solve a problem you might have.

We recommend searching Google Groups at http://groups.google.com for problems you're having with your phone. Be sure to include the following information when posting a question or searching for an answer:

- **Your phone model:** At the time this book was written, the only phone available was the G1 from T-Mobile.

- **Your mobile provider:** This is your service company, such as T-Mobile or AT&T.

- **The applications you have installed:** Many problems are caused by one particular application. By including a list of the applications you have installed, you make it easier for people to help you.

If you have a question about anything you've read in this book, feel free to email the authors at googonthego@gmail.com.

Index

FREE Online Edition

Your purchase of **Google on the Go: Using an Android-Powered Mobile Phone** includes access to a free online edition for 45 days through the Safari Books Online subscription service. Nearly every Que book is available online through Safari Books Online, along with more than 5,000 other technical books and videos from publishers such as Addison-Wesley Professional, Cisco Press, Exam Cram, IBM Press, O'Reilly, Prentice Hall, and Sams.

SAFARI BOOKS ONLINE allows you to search for a specific answer, cut and paste code, download chapters, and stay current with emerging technologies.

Activate your FREE Online Edition at www.informit.com/safarifree

> **STEP 1:** Enter the coupon code: DGNUIVH.

> **STEP 2:** New Safari users, complete the brief registration form.
> Safari subscribers, just log in.

If you have difficulty registering on Safari or accessing the online edition, please e-mail customer-service@safaribooksonline.com